NEVER HIT THE SNOOZE BUTTON

NEVER HIT THE Snooze BUTTON

Why The Little Things Matter—
And Why You Should Care

Joey Jenkins

OPTIMAL IMPACT GROUP

Beaverton, Oregon

Optimal Impact Group
Beaverton, Oregon 97008

Line editing by Indigo: Editing, Design, and More
Book design by Chris Rurik

Printed in the United States of America

ISBN 978-0-692-13352-1

To my beloved parents for giving me a strong foundation of love and support.

To my incredible brothers who have always believed in me and encouraged me through the down times. I'm still in the game because of you.

To my greatest mentor, Troy Snow, for being there for me during my darkest moments and for guiding me through my deepest trials.

CONTENTS

Foreword

"If one of you says to them, 'Go in peace; keep warm and well fed,' but does nothing about their physical needs, what good is it?"

—James 2:16, New International Version Bible

EVERY NOW AND THEN, we are graced with extraordinary personalities that the world has never seen, and will never see again. People who leave the world wildly different than how they found it. You know them when you see them. They become household names, you learn about them in school, and it's not because they seek the attention, but because we seek them. You can identify them by their unwavering grit, their readiness to sacrifice everything in pursuit of what's right, and their willingness to take on overwhelming burdens for the benefit of others. They get us through the hard times—they inspire us to do more and be more. When others crave money, fame, and notoriety, they seek impact as much as a man stranded in a scorching desert desires a cold glass of water. There is something special about them, though they would never admit it themselves.

So it is my honor to tell you, as one of Joey's closest friends, business collaborators, and the director of his award-winning documentary, *Perception: From Prison to Purpose*, that Joey Jenkins is one of those people. I know this firsthand because I am also one of his greatest success stories.

When I was eighteen, I was set up to have everything I ever wanted. I graduated high school with an associate's degree. I was a competitive athlete and starting my own business while entering my last two years in college. But after a series of personal tragedies and health challenges, any chance I thought I had of becoming the best version of myself seemed to be gone. After repeated attempts at getting myself back and failing, I became discouraged and eventually resentful. I had spun a complicated web of excuses, justifications, and fears that had a firm hold of me and wouldn't let go. I was in a dangerous spiral with no end in sight, until I met Joey.

We met when he was working at a fitness center and set up my membership. A process that normally takes ten to fifteen minutes turned into an hour-long conversation about life and health. We met again a year later through our mutual friend, Lamar Hurd. They were both planning a trip to Haiti with their respective nonprofit organizations, and I was invited to produce a documentary about the trip. I got to see firsthand the profound impact Joey's nonprofit organization, Ncompass, had on the orphans in this extremely impoverished village in Haiti. In the evenings we would stay up and talk about how this impact could be expanded all over the globe, how inspiring others to become givers was the most effective way to make real impact, and what we felt our life's purpose was. It was around this time that Joey decided he would quit his job at the fitness center and dedicate his life, full-time, to his mission. We started meeting more regularly and quickly became close friends.

We shared many values and ambitions. I wanted to help people just as much as he did, but one setback and failure after another had left me a shell of the person I was before with no clue how to get back. Joey was convinced, however, that I could still have the life I wanted. He saw a potential in me that I could no longer see myself, and when Joey sees even the tiniest glimpse of light, he charges through like a bull and never looks back.

Joey doesn't just give advice and coaching sessions—he gets in the trenches with you. You are now a team fighting together. This is where you see Joey's warrior spirit. This is evident in his relentless commitment to staying in shape by standards usually reserved for Olympic athletes. When most people see challenges and obstacles in the way, they retreat, or at the very least complain; Joey smiles. Challenges are his best friend. He sees them as opportunities for greatness—not for his greatness, but for yours and mine.

As Joey and I worked together on reversing my years of limiting beliefs and pessimism, my problems became his problems. My wins became his wins. I think he was more determined to get me to a better place than I was. We would text literally every day, set up scorecards to track my progress, and meet on short notice virtually any time I needed it. And this was at a time where he was regularly working sixty-hour weeks. For a time, we would meet every Monday morning at 6:00 a.m. for a jog to a local coffee shop to make sure we got our week off to a good start.

Little by little, I started getting better. I started believing in myself again. He poured so much belief and optimism into me that it became contagious. The overall approach was relatively simple. Whenever I was discouraged or not sure if I was heading fast enough in the right direction, he would repeat, "Sometimes, direction is more important than perfection." So simple but so true. By keeping the big picture alive, but focusing on the little things that will actually get you there, you become inspired to keep going, winning, and achieving until, slowly, you look back and find you're already there.

And that's where I find myself today. For the first time since I was eighteen, I'm actually optimistic about the future. I have been finally achieving things on par with my ambitions again and am slated to have even more in the near future. For this I give complete credit to Joey. He has been the most impactful friend I have ever had, and I truly hope you give him the chance to be that for you as well.

I tell you my story because I really want you to know that although the journey can be so hard and may seem impossible at times, believe me, it is not. Sometimes you need someone to tell you that over and over again until you believe it yourself. The secret ingredient to Joey's effectiveness is not just that he helps you believe, but he also helps you identify an inspiring vision, formulate a concrete strategy, and develop a step-by-step action plan for achieving it. He will help you appreciate the power and magic of the little things, the crucial importance of using consistency to build exponential growth and impact, the vital importance of commitment to your goals and to others, and a measurable way to chart your success and milestones so you can see tangible evidence of your progress.

And lastly, there is no one better to celebrate your wins with than Joey, because he understands the vital importance that small actions have on your long-term results. Therefore, he treats any small victories you have as monumental achievements—and if you really think about it, they are. Which is why he greatly appreciates the fact that you have picked up this book. He spent almost five years grinding it out, reading hundreds of books, watching countless TED Talks, giving a TEDx speech himself, traveling around the world, and giving up nights and weekends to develop and perfect the ideas and principles for this book. He did not do that for what he will get out of it, he did it for you.

Joey knows that you can become your best self and that if you are committed, your best days are ahead of you. I have seen Joey bring out the absolute best in so many people, and I can say from experience, he will absolutely do the same for you. If you are a big dreamer and are ready to put the work into the little things that will help you get there, then get ready for a journey, because the pages that follow can be the ones that change the rest of your life.

—Jonathan Reed

Acknowledgments

I WOULD LIKE TO EXPRESS my sincere gratitude to the people who helped bring this book to life.

First of all, I would like to thank my beautiful wife, Stephanie, for always being my rock. Your steadfast love and support are the reason I am able to do what I do. I would also like to thank our three amazing children, Lucy, Joshua, and Andrew, for sacrificing nights of wrestling with Dad so I could take time to produce this book.

I would like to thank all the people who provided support through editing, strategy, and valuable feedback. Thank you to Jake Rosenberg, Jocelyn Kuhn, Pete Jones, Chris Jenkins, Rich Jenkins, Cassie Parry, Noah Schultz, Scott Engler, Gary Hough, Tracey Beagle, Miles Dodge, Patty Perez, Kristen Hall-Geisler, and Vinnie Kinsella.

I would like to extend special thanks to Ali McCart Shaw from Indigo: Editing, Design, and More for being the primary editor for the entire manuscript. I recently heard the quote by Stephen King, "To write is human, to edit is divine." After writing my first book, I realize how true this is, and I am blown away by Ali's gifting as an editor.

I would like to thank Lionheart Coffee Company in Beaverton, Oregon for providing me with a beautiful location to write as well as the best customer service in town.

A big thank you to my design team. Thank you to Chris Rurik for handling the design process from start to finish. Thank you to Jonathan Reed and Travis Madison for my cover design and for being patient through countless iterations.

Lastly, I would like to thank Jonathan Reed again for writing a beautiful foreword to the book and for being my most supportive friend through my grueling entrepreneurial journey. I would have quit countless times without you in my corner.

Introduction

"Do you love life? Then do not squander time, for that's the stuff life is made of."

—Benjamin Franklin

WHAT DOES IT MEAN to hit the snooze button? It used to mean flopping your arm onto your bedside table and fumbling to hit a plastic rectangular spot on your clock radio. Now, it likely means a swipe of your finger across the screen of your smartphone, which is now fully charged, screaming mindlessly at you, and glowing in the pre-dawn dark of your bedroom. That's what it means, physically speaking, to hit the snooze button. But to me, it means much more.

First (and I will argue, *foremost*) it's how you start your day. In that first waking moment of each new morning, it's your first decision. Sure, you're probably groggy when you make that decision, and you might even regret making it when you're stuck in traffic and stressed about getting to work on time. But you make it—you hit the snooze button and steal nine minutes from your waking life. It's just a little arm flop, a finger swipe. A reflex, an instant reaction, maybe even an involuntary muscular twitch. You might tell yourself that while it might mean *something*, it's such a little thing in the grand scheme of your life that it *can't* mean much.

I disagree. Few metaphors represent the power and magic of the little things better than the idea of the snooze button. If hitting the snooze button is the first action you take every day, then this action is setting the tone for the rest of your day. If you hit that button, it's the first impression you choose to give yourself. Pressing that button impresses, like a fingerprint, a mark upon your day. And this mark is one of procrastination. As Ben Franklin indicated in the quote above, to squander time is to squander life. *Will you squander your life?* That's the question the snooze button asks you each and every morning. And each morning—like it or not—you have to answer it.

As you can tell from the title of this book, I don't think you should hit that button! I think you should take that chance each morning to affirm that you're not going to squander *today*. It has to become a habit. Each morning, you have the chance to either tell yourself you are someone who does what you say you're going to do—or you are someone who doesn't. To snooze or not to snooze— when you refuse to hit the button, you tell yourself that today will not be a wasted day. Not hitting the button is telling yourself you love life and you won't squander it. And what we tell ourselves each day and in every situation matters a great deal!

When I was twenty years old, I decided I wanted to write a book called *Never Hit the Snooze Button*. I had begun to realize the power and importance of the little things and how large a role they play in every aspect of our lives. I had started to learn this lesson through my college job at Oregon State University's recreation center. I worked with many other college students cleaning the facility, check- ing people into the gym, and renting out equipment. As I performed my job, I began to notice that small differences in employees' actions made a huge difference over time in their success and impact in the job. One employee would simply smile at every member entering the facility, while another just checked them in with a straight face. One employee would clean all thirty pieces of equipment required on a shift, while another would fall short and clean just twenty-five. One person would show up on time consistently, while another employee would routinely be one or two minutes late.

At first the difference was negligible and didn't stand out. But over the course of the year, I noticed that the employees who did the little things well stood out head and shoulders above the rest. They were appreciated, rewarded, recognized, and promoted, and they made a significant difference in the lives of other employees and our members. The other employees, however, didn't develop meaningful relationships, and simply cashed a paycheck.

As I started seeing this trend, I also started testing it, living it, and ultimately taking advantage of the small actions that add up over time. I started to notice the small things in life. Small things like the snooze button. I realized the snooze button was our first small act every day and that it was a powerful metaphor, and I believed it would make a great book one day.

However, like most, I hate watching hypocrisy, or even worse, being guilty of it myself. And while I understood the power of this metaphor, and was beginning to do the little things in many areas of life, I simply couldn't seem to stop hitting that menacing button on my alarm clock. I was a snooze-button junkie and spent the next nine years falling off the wagon and jumping back on. Like someone struggling with a drug addiction (which I have witnessed closely), I would bounce back and forth all the time. I'd be snooze-button clean for three months, and then I'd fall off for two. Back and forth I went for nine whole years!

I never lost my desire to stop hitting the snooze button, but ultimately, I learned it all boils down to the idea that habits and systems always beat intentions. It is the habits and systems we create to manage our intentions that actually determine how we behave.

This is a challenging lesson to learn, though, and many of us still haven't internalized it and therefore continually live a life far removed from our ideal life, ideal integrity, and ideal values. As theologian Nathaniel Emmons says, "Habit is either the best of servants or the worst of masters."

I believe one of the main aspects that separate the most successful people from the majority is their acceptance that intentions aren't enough. Once we realize this, we become willing to integrate systems and processes into our lives to manage our habits and therefore drive results we never thought possible. I have spent the past decade as a coach, consultant, nonprofit director, and public speaker. I have had the privilege of working with peak performers in the business and nonprofit worlds as well as with individuals striving to accomplish huge dreams. I have also spent years working with prison inmates, the homeless, and children in Haiti who have either lost their parents or were abandoned by them. Through these diverse experiences, I have seen time and again the magic of the little things, and how they can and will change our lives, whether we like it or not.

In this short book, I have two simple goals:

1. Convince you that the little things matter and the stakes are higher than you think.
2. Show you how to take control over the small, seemingly insignificant details so you can live the life you desire, become the person you were made to be, and achieve your maximum impact in the world.

To do this effectively, this book will have two parts. The first part will address the *why*. Once you know why something is important—and believe in it enough—the *how* becomes much easier. I start with the *why* because I believe the small choices and actions we make every day have a much larger effect on who we become and what impact we leave on this world than we think. The second part of the book addresses the *how* and supplies you with the practical tools and systems needed to consistently take action. Throughout each section you will occasionally find worksheets designed to help you reframe your thinking or implement new actions or systems into your life. Please don't skip these exercises as they are a critical component to your success.

While chapters will occasionally speak specifically to the snooze button, this book is about so much more than that. Therefore, I am not going to connect every example or story to it. But it is always in the undercurrent. If you honestly bought this book just to figure out how to stop hitting the snooze button, it should deliver, but I hope it does a whole lot more for you as well. If you finish this book and still can't figure out how to stop hitting the snooze button, give me a call and I'll help you create a simple game plan to be successful. I've included my number in the back of the book.

I believe time is our most precious asset and that we need to use it wisely. I don't take for granted the time you are choosing to devote to this book, and I am incredibly grateful for your trust that I will deliver value to you. I take that trust seriously and will do my best to be of service to you through the following chapters. Thank you for reading!

—Joey Jenkins

PART ONE

Why the Little Things Matter

Setting the Tone

"A journey of a thousand miles starts with one step."

—Lao Tzu

COACHES AND TEACHERS UNDERSTAND how important setting the tone early is. The standards you uphold in that first week of practice or class will make all the difference through the rest of the season and year. It will determine how your athletes or students view you and how you operate as a team and approach the year together. The snooze button represents how you internally set the tone for your day. It can seep into all areas of your life without you even knowing it. It is absolutely critical that you set the tone early and strong!

Our entire lives are filled with important firsts. People will tell you how important first impressions are—how important your answer to that first interview question at that potential new job is, how important your first day of practice is as you join the new team. First impressions are hard to shake. It's human nature that once we have made a judgment of someone, it takes a whole lot of effort and time to reshape that judgment. Firsts matter. The snooze button is your personal first each day. It is the first impression you give yourself each day about the kind of person you are and the kind of day you are going to have. Most successful peo-

The snooze button is your personal first each day.

ple understand the importance of firsts, which is why most highly successful people have some habitual morning routine they do before anything else. The following are a few examples.

Michelle Gass, Former President of Starbucks

For over fifteen years, Michelle has woken up each morning at 4:30 a.m. to go running. She believes her morning routine has helped boost her happiness and business success. (No snooze button here.)

Steve Jobs, Former CEO of Apple

The late Steve Jobs spent his mornings reevaluating his work and desires. In his speech to the 2005 graduating class at Stanford, Jobs said, "For the past 33 years, I have looked in the mirror every morning and asked myself: 'If today were the last day of my life, would I want to do what I am about to do today?' And whenever the answer has been 'no' for too many days in a row, I know I need to change something."

Tony Robbins, Motivational Speaker and Life Coach

Tony Robbins helps motivate people to become better leaders and achieve greater success. He says that the moment that changed his life was when he decided he wasn't living up to his standard so he changed his habits and way of thinking. His advice is to do an Hour of Power every morning, which includes motivational sayings, visualization, and exercise.

The Hour of Power can come in many forms. You can find plenty of examples with a simple Google search. After over a decade of studying Tony Robbins's work, I have crafted my own Hour of Power to start my day off right. Here is my current routine, which I am always tweaking to make more effective for my current season of life:

Morning Routine
1. Drink a large glass of water.
2. Read Bible, pray, or worship.
3. Read my top three Wildly Important Goals for the year (based on Sean Covey's *The Four Disciplines of Execution*).
4. Stretch while watching Brian Johnson's Optimize + 1 videos.
5. Do one set of push-ups, pull-ups, and plank.
6. Take morning supplements.
7. Perform ten slow, deep breaths.
8. Fill out my morning routine worksheet. (See figure 1.)
9. Unload the dishwasher.
10. Take out the trash and recycling.
11. Read this excerpt from the Navy Seal Ethos:

> *"I will never quit. I persevere and thrive on adversity. My Nation expects me to be physically harder and mentally stronger than my enemies. If knocked down, I will get back up, every time. I will draw on every remaining ounce of strength to protect my teammates and to accomplish our mission. I am never out of the fight."*

I read this to motivate me to raise my standards, and who better to model after than the Navy Seals?

I don't always get to do this morning routine, but I do most days. And the days I do it definitely feel different than the days I don't. I feel more energetic, more focused, and less stressed about the challenges of the day when I do my full Hour of Power in the morning. I

What are my primary goals for today?

1. _____
2. _____
3. _____

"It's not enough to be busy; so are the ants. The question is: what are we busy about?"
—Henry David Thoreau

What emotion am I going to amplify today?

1. _____

What three things am I most thankful for this morning?

1. _____
2. _____
3. _____

What two affirmations do I need to write, read, or say this morning?

1. _____
2. _____

How am I going to have more *fun* today?

1. _____

Who am I going to bless the most today?

1. _____

Figure 1: *Morning Routine*

also typically exercise in the morning after my Hour of Power. This means on the days I want to start work at 8:00 a.m., I need to wake up at 5:00 a.m. to make all of this happen. Just to be clear, the primary idea of this book is not about waking up early. While I am personally a morning person, and believe there is value in getting up early, the snooze button to me represents our personal integrity of sticking to our commitments and doing the little things well.

How We Start Matters

As I am writing this, I have a documentary team working hard on editing the beginning of a prison transformation documentary that my company, Optimal Impact Group, produced. I began working with the Oregon Youth Authority a few years ago to help incarcerated men eighteen to twenty-four years old. One young man named Noah Schultz stood out immediately. During his seven-and-a-half-year sentence, he graduated high school and college, self-published two poetry books, did a TEDx Talk, and started a nonprofit to help troubled teens. In the forty-minute film, the production team perfectly captured Noah's story and his powerful example of transformation, hope, and second chances. However, the introduction didn't have a strong enough hook until at least three minutes in. In today's society, if people aren't hooked by three minutes, you've lost them. We spent countless hours reworking the introduction to ensure that it draws you in right from the start, because we know that if we don't, we lose you forever and the film doesn't provide the impact we desire.

When I am prepping for speaking engagements, one of the areas I spend the most time on is the introduction. Not only is this your first impression to your audience, but nailing the introduction also gives you the confidence that will carry you through the rest of your talk. You have to know your intro inside and out and practice this section more than any other.

As a life, leadership, and business coach, I know my very first meeting with a new client is essential. I have hired and worked with

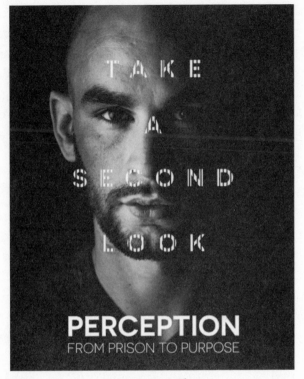

Poster of our film.

many coaches over the years. One coach I hired told me our first meeting would last two hours, as he was going to do a deep dive and really get to know me. The meeting ended up lasting thirty minutes, and he didn't ask me any questions about myself. Not the best first impression. Then he forgot about our second session. When you are paying $250 an hour, this doesn't leave you feeling very good. It's really hard to come back from that!

Setting the tone in life matters! It's why Admiral William H. McRaven drives this concept home so deeply in his book *Make Your Bed*. He points out the importance of starting our day off right with such a simple practice. His premise is that little things like this, add up over time, and can change your life, and maybe even the world. Author and speaker Mel Robbins also hones in on this concept in

Day of Noah's release from prison after seven and a half years! It was a beautiful Shawshank Redemption *moment.*

Documentary team celebrating Noah's release together.

her book *The 5 Second Rule*. She says, "There's actually a neurological reason why you should never, ever hit the snooze button...You know that getting a good night sleep is important for productivity, right? Well I bet you didn't know that how you wake up is not only as important, it's actually in some cases more important than how you sleep. Scientists have recently discovered that when you hit the snooze button, it has a negative impact on brain function and productivity that can last up to four hours. It's called sleep inertia." She goes on to explain that our sleep cycles typically take around 90-110 minutes. Around two hours before you wake up, your body shifts into a two-hour mode where it will slowly start to wake you up. If your alarm goes off and you hit the snooze button, your body kicks you back into another 90-110 minute sleep cycle. When you finally decide to wake up after hitting snooze, physically you are capable of getting out of bed, but mentally you can't shake yourself out of the sleep cycle you entered back into. As Robbins says, "You've now screwed yourself."

The saying "It's not how you start but how you finish" is inaccurate and misleading. It's not simply how you start or how you finish—it's how you run the entire race. For those of you who have run a marathon, has anyone ever asked you what your mile time was in your first or last mile? No one cares! All they want to know is how long the entire race took you. How hard did you push yourself through every mile combined? However, the way you start impacts how you run the rest of the race a great deal, which is why starting strong is critical.

Make sure you start every day well, because you never know how many days you have left. Don't let hitting the snooze button be how you set the tone for your day. You have the power to knock that habit out for the rest of your life!

"It's not where you start or where you finish... It's the distance you travel in life that matters most."
—Attributed to Greg Plitt

Key Chapter Takeaways:

1. The snooze button represents how you internally set the tone for your entire day. It can seep into all areas of your life without you even knowing it.
2. Most successful people understand the importance of firsts, which is why most highly successful people have a consistent morning routine.
3. The saying "It's not how you start but how you finish" is inaccurate and misleading. It's how you run the entire race in life that matters.

Life Is a Game of Inches

"There are no big things, only an accumulation of many little things."

—John Wooden

THIS CHAPTER IS INTENDED to remind those of you who, like me, understand the importance of the little things in life but occasionally need a reminder. It is also for those of you who may not yet fully understand the potential life-changing effects our daily choices and actions can and will have, whether we like it or not.

In the movie *Any Given Sunday*, Tony D'Amato (played by Al Pacino) is the coach of an NFL team aspiring for greatness. At one point in the movie, he gives a stirring pregame speech about how football and life are both a game of inches. "The inches we need are everywhere around us. They are in every break of the game, every minute, every second," he says. In his speech he demonstrates that life is a lot like football, in the fact that there are small, seemingly insignificant inches (small opportunities) all around us that we often don't even notice. Often times these small inches can determine whether we win or lose the football game, or win or lose in life. This speech impacted my life greatly! I have listened to that speech hundreds of times, with most coming on a three-hour drive across Oregon for my high school baseball team's state playoff game. I listened to it for three hours straight because it spoke to my heart and soul so deeply. My flag football team in college even had me recite pieces of it occasionally before games. I highly recommend you go watch it on YouTube right now.

Like most of you, though, I often haven't mastered the "inches" in all areas of my life as much as I desire to, but I definitely have an appreciation for their immense power and impact. Through a variety of life circumstances, I am well aware of how important the inches are in life.

One Degree of Difference

You may have heard the temperature metaphor used to demonstrate the importance of the little things. At 211 degrees, nothing happens to water, but if you simply turn the heat up one single degree, it changes everything and the water hits a roaring boil. It demonstrates the potential that inches play in our lives, while at the same time representing the challenge of living them consistently. Notice that when water goes from 137 degrees to 138 degrees, nothing noticeably different happens. When you go from 172 degrees to 173, the same pattern persists. But when you hit the boiling point, everything changes.

I have seen countless people struggle to find that boiling point, and in the process they stop thinking that the little things matter. Someone taught them that writing thank-you notes was important. They wrote thank-you notes for a few months, and nothing in their life changed, so they stopped. Someone told them walking thirty minutes a day could change their life, but after two months not enough was different, so they quit. A personal trainer or nutritionist made health and fitness recommendations, but they didn't get noticeable results after thirty days, so they gave it all up. We have all probably been guilty of this kind of thinking and behavior at some point.

I felt the effect of this one degree of difference powerfully and personally during my senior year of high school when my baseball team reached the quarterfinals of the state playoffs. It was the farthest our program had ever made it, and we believed we had a legitimate chance to win the state title.

Down by one run with two outs in the bottom of the sixth inning (high school baseball only has seven innings), I found myself in position to tie the score. My teammate then hit a beautiful line drive to left field, and I was off from second base! My nickname in high school was "The Jet" (hence my son's name: Joshua Jet Jenkins), so when I saw my coach wave me home, I activated every muscle, increased my effort, and went full out! I could see in the catcher's eyes that the left fielder must have made an amazing play with a perfect throw home, as he was eyeing the ball clearly close to his glove. I dove headfirst, and the below picture says it all.

Close but no cigar.

I was thrown out at home, and we went on to lose the game 1–0. I was devastated, but I have this picture framed on my desk to this day, sixteen years later, to remind me how important the inches are and how I fell short!

Now let me be very clear here. I did not feel guilty for getting thrown out because I didn't run my hardest or make a great dive home, because I did. I was not upset with the umpire for calling me out on a close call. I was upset with myself for losing the game in the off-season.

I lost that game for our team before I even stepped on the field. I lost that game over the summer when I was sitting on the couch eating Cool Ranch Doritos, drinking Capri Suns, watching *The Disney Afternoon*, and playing video games all day. I lost that game for our team because I didn't make the most of my potential. Was I still fast enough to be called "The Jet"? Yes. Was I still one of the hardest workers on the team once practice started? Yes. But did I fail to reach my full potential and achieve results I was capable of? Most definitely! There are no guarantees in life, and I can't promise that we would have won if I'd replaced every bag of Doritos in the summer with a sprint workout. But I could have been prouder of my effort and accomplishment, and who knows, maybe my team and I would have a state title to be proud of as well.

Guilt vs. Shame

I know what some of you are thinking: *Don't be so hard on yourself. It's not healthy to live with that level of guilt and that high of standards.* However, I can assure you it is not a guilt that makes me feel deep shame and a lack of self-worth. I personally believe it is a healthy level of regret that simply drives me to be more, do more, and become more the next time. In her book *Rising Strong*, Brené Brown does a fantastic job of articulating the difference between shame and guilt. She says, "The difference between shame and guilt lies in the way we talk to ourselves. Shame is a focus on self, while guilt is a focus on behavior. This is not just semantics. There's a huge difference between I *screwed up* (guilt) and I *am a screwup* (shame). The former is acceptance of our imperfect humanity. The latter is basically an indictment of our very existence."

I think the current American culture is giving rise to a generation (or more) of people who are told they should always feel good about themselves, regardless of their actions and behavior. I simply don't think that's true. When I make stupid comments to my wife, I feel a healthy level of guilt and regret, apologize to her, and try to be a better husband next time. When I fail in my job because of a lack of strategic focus and effort, I acknowledge the mistake and commit to doing better next time.

I would encourage you not to shrink back from looking at your faults and failures. Instead, *own* all the "inches" you have lost over the years. Some of you, like me, are not where you want to be in certain areas of life. Let's take a long, hard look in the mirror and see what part we have played in that. When we do that, it actually creates a deep sense of personal power, because if you are to blame for where you are in certain areas today, then that also means you have a great deal of influence over where you end up tomorrow.

> *Own all the "inches" you have lost over the years.*

Law of Rewards

I have been listening to Tony Robbins for fourteen years now (since I was twenty years old). I was in the midst of a deep, dark depression when I was twenty, heartbroken for the first time in my life. The first cut truly is the deepest! I remember lying on the couch and seeing this silly infomercial come on about this passionate, giant man saying he could change my life. Well, when you are in a state of utter desperation, even if you are insanely frugal (which I am), then you take out your wallet and cough up over $300 for seven CDs that will, hopefully, help you survive, and maybe, if you are lucky, thrive. Now, there are no magic bullets, and I know there are plenty of people out there who are not Tony Robbins fans, and that's fine. But he truly has been one of the most inspirational and impactful people in my life.

All that's to say, of the thousands of dollars I have spent on his products and conferences over the years, my favorite teaching of his is about the Law of Rewards. In an hour-long CD titled *Power Talk!: Raising Your Standards*, Tony breaks down the way society rewards people. To summarize, he explains that typically in life we expect to be rewarded according to the level of work we put in, but it doesn't usually turn out that way. When people give poor work in life, they expect poor rewards. But in our society, when you do poor work, you get fired, you lose your marriage, or you have a heart attack. The results are worse than poor—they are awful! (It's important to acknowledge that not all of these always come from poor work. Often divorce is not someone's fault, or a heart attack is unavoidable, etc.)

Most of us don't do poor work, though—most of us do good work. And when we do good work, we expect good rewards, but unfortunately, we end up with poor rewards. This one isn't hard to prove. The majority of society does work they consider to be good, and the majority of society feels underappreciated, undervalued, and underpaid. We hear it all the time. This is the space where most people live: constantly frustrated by the feeling that they deserve more!

Then there are those few, driven individuals who give excellent work, and when they give excellent work, you would think, *they'd get rewarded for being one of the best*. However, even at the level of excellence, many still receive rewards one level below their effort. Which is why, often, many people who do excellent work only last a short time. It is hard to do excellent work, deliver more than most of your peers, relentlessly develop yourself, exceed expectations, and still be undervalued and underappreciated. I would relate this challenge back to the water boiling metaphor mentioned earlier. When you are working incredibly hard and you get the water temperature up to 205 degrees, often times the challenge of not seeing a roaring boil can be discouraging to the point of getting us to finally give in, lower our standards and stop living with the healthy habits that will eventually boil the water.

Robbins encourages us that there is still one final level. While it may be a huge jump between poor work, good work, and excellent work, the final level is actually only a few inches above excellent. It is the level called outstanding. It is the level where you *stand out* from all the rest. It is the level where the water finally hits the roaring boil, and you get *all the rewards!*

Many of you, like me, may be thinking that this is unfair and not the way society should reward people. Whether we like it or not though, certain principles stand fast and hold true regardless. We would be better off embracing the reality, and striving to live outstanding lives to receive rewards and impact worthy of our efforts.

Robbins goes on to demonstrate this concept by using the Olympics as an example. Millions of people gather around their televisions every two years to watch the most outstanding athletes in the world compete to see who truly stands out the most. And after years of ruthless discipline and focus, these athletes put their skills to the test. How do we reward the fourth-fastest person in the 100-meter dash? The fourth-fastest person in the world? We give them nothing except the experience and memory of the loss. How about the second-fastest person in the world? They may have only lost by hundredths of a second in the hundred-meter dash, but all they get is the silver medal, which is probably worth a few thousand dollars. Now compare that to how we reward the most outstanding person. We give them a gold medal, they get million-dollar endorsements, and we make them a hero for life! Their rewards are exponential compared to the next person in line, but the work difference was often times minimal.

Here's a more tangible example to prove the point. According to CNBC, in 2015 the average S&P 500 CEO (CEOs of the largest companies in the world) made $12.4 million, or 335 times the average pay of a rank-and-file employee within the company. Do you think the CEO is working 335 times harder than their average employee? No way! Society doesn't care. It doesn't matter that it isn't fair, they still receive compensation far above and beyond everyone else. While the CEO certainly isn't working 335 times harder than the average employee, I would be willing to bet that the majority of the time, he/she was winning the inches and doing the little things differently for a couple decades prior to earning that position.

This is not a political statement. This is simply showing you how our society rewards people. Once you understand this, and if you can accept it, then you can take action on it. You can embrace the truth that small acts over time add up to produce exponential rewards and results.

I have seen this play out for me in my personal career too. Prior to starting my own company, there was only one job I can confidently, without reservation, say I consistently delivered outstanding work ethic and commitment: during my undergrad years at Oregon State University when I worked at the recreation center. I loved my boss, my coworkers, and our members dearly. I was 100 percent committed to making that place the best it could be. I gave all I had every day for that facility and those people in the three years I worked there, and I was rewarded well. I received far more than I ever gave and was thanked, appreciated, developed, refined, and poured into like no other time of my life. My leadership and character grew in those three years more than it had in the rest of my life combined.

Fast-forward three years to my time working for a prominent fitness chain. I wavered back and forth between good and excellent commitment. I didn't believe in the company, its values, or its executive leaders. I didn't think it had an exciting and compelling vision, nor was I excited to give my heart and soul to the company. Every once in a while, I would remind myself that I should be working for God and not man (Colossians 3:23) and should always give my best self no matter where I am working. I would remind myself that I should work in any company as if my grandpa had founded it, because that is how I believe we should all work no matter where we are.

For a number of reasons, however, I failed to deliver to my own standards, and during my three-year tenure working for that company, like most employees, I felt undervalued and underappreciated. It was easy for me to blame everyone else for this, but ultimately, it was 100 percent my fault. I had not integrated my deep understanding of how society rewards us, and it cost me years of results and standards I wish I could do over.

So whether you are living your dream career or working through a season of transition and development, I encourage you to give all you have no matter what! It will pay off in the end. Same with your marriage, friendships, parenting, health, and all other areas of life. As motivational speaker Stephen C. Hogan once said, "You can't have a million-dollar dream with a minimum-wage work ethic."

The snooze button is just one inch. It is not a magic bullet—it won't get you that promotion or pay raise overnight. No one is going to come knocking at your door to reward you instantly for it. It is simply one inch in a long line of potential inches that all add up and make a difference in the end. Two of my favorite books ever are *The Slight Edge* by Jeff Olson and *The Compound Effect* by Darren Hardy. Both of those books demonstrate the reality of how small actions compound over time and produce massive results in the end. The results don't start showing up immediately, or even in the first few years or decade sometimes. Most people don't have the patience for the compound effect to serve them in a positive way in their life, and therefore they miss out on all the tremendous benefits it brings. Whether you believe that or not, whether you take action or not, is up to you. Either way, the compound effect is either going to work for you or against you, it is never neutral.

I will close this chapter with a Lao Tzu quote that exemplifies the importance of how the inches matter, even starting with our thoughts.

"Watch your thoughts; they become words.
Watch your words; they become actions.
Watch your actions; they become habits.
Watch your habits; they become character.
Watch your character; it becomes your destiny."
—Lao Tzu

Key Chapter Takeaways:

1. At 211 degrees, nothing happens to water, but if you simply turn the heat up one single degree, it changes everything and the water hits a roaring boil.
2. Society will always reward you at one level below the effort you put in—unless you deliver outstanding work. When you do that, you get *all the rewards!*
3. The snooze button is just one inch. Breaking the habit to hit it is not a magic bullet—it won't get you that promotion or pay raise overnight. No one is going to come knocking at your door to reward you instantly for it. It is simply one inch in a long line of potential inches that all add up and make a difference in the end.

The Magic Is in the Little Things

"We cannot all do great things, but we can do small things with great love."

—Mother Teresa

NOT ONLY DO THE RESULTS come from the little things in life, but so does the magic. Often we are so consumed with grandiose goals that we miss the beauty all around us all of the time; I know I do. Social worker and nun, Mother Teresa said, "We shall never know all the good that a simple smile can do." How true! A simple smile can be a game changer. I think it is devastating how much beauty I miss all around me every day simply because I forget to notice. In one of my favorite books, *The Alchemist*, author Paulo Coelho says it best, "When each day is the same as the next, it's because people fail to recognize the good things that happen in their lives every day that the sun rises." Each day is filled with an overwhelming amount of beauty if we would but open our eyes to its existence.

Not only do the results come from the little things in life, but so does the magic.

When I was twenty-one, I met a girl named Kate. We started dating and I fell in love fast. We talked about our hopes and dreams, we talked about impacting the world by starting a nonprofit someday, and we even opened a bank account together to start raising money for it. I thought I was going to marry her and that she was my soul mate. Then one night, during the summer of 2005, Kate was killed in a tragic car accident. I was devastated! I had never experienced such extreme pain in my life and immediately knew I had just entered a valley that was deeper and longer than any I had ever walked through before. It was overwhelming to say the least.

A few days after Kate's death, I went to Las Vegas with my best friend to celebrate his twenty-first birthday. It was a trip we had been planning since sixth grade, so I couldn't bail on him, even though Vegas was the last thing on my mind. I still remember the flight clearly. I remember hoping the plane would crash and put me out of my misery. That was not a healthy thought, nor was it considerate of everyone else on the plane at the time, but I was in a dark place and all I could think about was escaping the severe pain.

When we arrived, the trip was much more drab for me than I had imagined. While my friend played the roulette table all night long, I was aimlessly wandering the streets of Las Vegas at three in the morning. I vividly remember walking into a tie shop and meandering around to pass the time. What happened next is a vague memory, but I still remember exactly how it made me feel.

The shopkeeper interacted with me, and whatever he said or however he said it gave me hope that life would turn out okay. He didn't say anything profound, and he didn't know what I was going through at all, but something about his smile and the words he said refreshed my soul in a time of deep desperation. American poet, Maya Angelou is often credited with saying, "I've learned that people will forget what you said, people will forget what you did, but people will never forget how you made them feel." What I remember about that interaction is that his name was Bob, his face was kind, and he made me feel at peace in the midst of a dark storm. It truly is the little things.

I remember another time ordering a hamburger at a restaurant called Nearly Normal's in Corvallis, Oregon. When the server brought my burger out, it had my name written in ketchup on the inside of my bun. I was blown away and thought that was the coolest customer service move I had seen. I went back to that restaurant solely because they did that. Often it is the "little things" that stand out the most.

How many times have you received a phone call, text message, or letter in a time of need that gave you the courage to continue? I hope you can clearly recollect moments in your life when this happened. As I write this, I am flooded with too many stories to share of powerful moments when another person's encouragement and simple words were magical and gave me the strength I needed to continue through the hard times.

I keep a survival box, which a dear friend of mine created for me in college. In the box, I keep special messages from meaningful people in my life. The box is overflowing with words of encouragement that I pull out and read when I am discouraged. Leadership is tough and can take you to raw and difficult spaces. In the times I am thinking about throwing in the towel, sometimes reading a simple note from five or ten years ago goes a long way!

The night before my first paid speaking gig was another time I was quite nervous and overwhelmed. I was up late practicing and refining my talk when I decided to take a break and check the mail. In it was a letter from a dear friend in New York who, without knowing I had my upcoming talk, just felt like sending me some encouragement with a wristband that said, *Whatever It Takes*. Needless to say, I was re-energized and ready to roll!

"Kind words are short and easy to speak, but their echoes are truly endless."

—Mother Teresa

Encouraging letter and wristband from my friend in my time of need.

Crank Up the Music

I am a huge believer in dreaming big! I am all about having God-sized dreams that seem impossible to everyone around you. It is why I admire Elon Musk, founder of Tesla and SpaceX, so much! I love hearing about his dreams of colonizing Mars and ending our reliance on gas-guzzling cars. At the same time, though, it is important to never lose the perspective that mountaineer Harold Melchart points out: "Live your life each day as you would climb a mountain. An occasional glance toward the summit keeps the goal in mind, but many beautiful scenes are to be observed from each new vantage point." There is so much beauty around us every single day. Don't miss it!

The Magic Is in the Little Things

My wife and I just finished season one of the show *This Is Us*. One of the characters gives these words of wisdom to his son on how to live: "Roll all your windows down, Randall. Crank up the music."

Life is short, don't let it pass you by! Don't hit the snooze button and miss what this brief life has to offer you. Think of all the beautiful actions you could take with that extra nine minutes in the morning. Here are a few ideas:

1. Write your kids, spouse, or a friend an encouraging note about what you love about them, highlighting some of their special gifts and abilities.
2. Think of one mini-adventure you have been wanting to take for years, and plan it for sometime in the next six months.
3. Watch Drew Dudley's TEDx Talk called "Everyday Leadership." It's less than seven minutes and will inspire you to realize the potential that small actions can have.
4. Create a survival box—a simple container to store encouraging notes from friends, family, or coworkers that you can refer back to during hard times.
5. Create a "Cell Phone Daycare"—a place to put your phone when you walk in the door at home so you can stay focused on being present and engaged with your family during dinner or beyond (this concept is credited to Taylor Smith).

"If you think you are too small to make a difference, try sleeping with a mosquito."
—Dalai Lama

Cell Phone Daycare example.

Key Chapter Takeaways:

1. As Mother Teresa pointed out, a simple smile can go a long way in life. Little things make all the difference.
2. Sometimes a simple letter, phone call, or text message is all someone needs to give them the courage to continue and stay in the fight. Don't miss those opportunities to encourage another human being each day.
3. Life is short, roll down your windows, crank up the music, and enjoy every minute of it.

Consistency Is King

"If you will spend an extra hour each day of study in your chosen field, you will be a national expert in that field in five years or less."

—Earl Nightingale

MOST FAILURE BOILS DOWN to a lack of consistency. Everyone can verbally articulate their understanding of the importance of consistency, but many of us can't seem to integrate it deeply into our subconscious understanding and belief system. Gary Vaynerchuk, author, speaker, and digital marketer, does an amazing job of demonstrating this in his video "Overnight Success." It is a must-watch! Go YouTube it now. (Warning: He uses explicit language, but the content is worth it.) In his eight-minute video, he shows so clearly how important consistency is and how there really are no overnight successes. Someone may become big overnight, but there were usually years, even decades, of work behind the scenes that you didn't get to see.

As I write this, Vaynerchuk has a net worth of over $160 million and his company VaynerMedia has over 600 employees. In this video he shows us that before he became a so-called overnight success, he made over a thousand videos for Wine Library TV. He didn't expect overnight success, so he kept pushing year after year, video after video, until he hit his breakthrough. To be successful, you need to figure out what strategy will get you the results you desire, and then be consistent in implementing that strategy. It's really that simple when you boil it all down. However, simple doesn't mean easy.

I recently did a podcast interview with Anthony Trucks; former NFL athlete and current business coach and national speaker. He has achieved very high levels of success, and in our interview, he talked about the role that consistency played in helping him achieve breakthrough. Every night he films what he calls his *Nightly 90*. It is a ninety-second video in which he motivates, encourages, and challenges his audience. At the time of this writing, he had over 240,000 Facebook followers and growing! He made hundreds of these videos with very little engagement before he finally broke through. In our interview, he had filmed around 750 clips (now over 1,150) of his *Nightly 90* without skipping a day! It took about 350 in a row before he finally started to break through and see real results. Patience is the game, folks. You have to find a way to commit, stay the course, and be consistent.

Our society loves intensity but lacks consistency. At an early age, we learn to prioritize one but not the other, and we turn that into our habitual lifestyle approach. We cram for tests with intensity because we didn't attend class or study with consistency. I did this myself all the way through my junior year in college, when I finally realized that if I simply showed up for class every time, paid attention, and did the work along the way, I could actually get better results in the same or less time. Intensity is great, but consistency is king!

Discipline and Consistency

What if you didn't choose one or the other—consistency or intensity—but prioritized both? What would that do for your results?

What would it do for your relationships? What would it do for your impact? I believe it would change everything for you! Actor Denzel Washington said, "Between goals and achievement are discipline and consistency." If you want achievement, you can't pass over discipline and consistency. It just won't happen without them. Discipline and consistency are great ways to differentiate yourself because they are so unsexy. There is nothing appealing about them. Trust me, it's a lot easier to sell the book titled *Get Rich Without Working* than one titled *Never Hit the Snooze Button*. One promises ease while the other calls for dedication.

> *Intensity is great, but consistency is king!*

Author and motivational speaker Jim Rohn beautifully expresses it in his statement, "We must all suffer from one of two pains: the pain of discipline or the pain of regret. The difference is discipline weighs ounces while regret weighs tons." I hope this point drives deep into your psyche! This is such a powerful truth that can literally change everything if you let it. Open your eyes and look around you. If you look closely enough, you will find countless people walking around with huge burdens of regret they are carrying. These are people who didn't understand this principle and were unwilling to suffer the pain of discipline, which pales in comparison to the pain of regret they now carry.

Habits and Routines

Leadership coach and author John Maxwell said, "You'll never change your life until you change something you do daily. The secret of your success is found in your daily routine." If you study successful people (which you should), this concept will rise to the surface over and over again! All the greats understand the power of habit. Go read Charles Duhigg's book *The Power of Habit*, and you will discover that it is our habits and daily routines that end up shaping our destiny.

Habits are so difficult to master because they don't produce instant results, and we are surrounded by an instant-results and instant-gratification culture. We expect six-minute abs and microwaveable nutrition. Unfortunately, this is not typical in reality. The problem with habits is that they are methodical and slow to produce results. They do produce with almost certainty, but they are seeds you plant and wait patiently to see grow. Farmers understand this concept well, as they cultivate land for long periods of time before harvesting the crop and seeing a return on their investment. The rest of us have lost the gift of patience that the farmer embodies.

We start a new habit of drinking a hundred ounces of water a day, and when we don't feel transformed after two weeks, we give it up and search for another silver bullet. Maybe walking thirty minutes a day will do the trick? Two weeks later, we give that up and search for a third habit, and we get stuck in the crazy cycle over and over again. This is why a new superfood becomes so prominent every year or two. People are hoping it is the magic bullet to fix all their health issues. You will hear about apple cider vinegar for a while, then goji berries, acai berries, or pine nuts. We constantly cycle through habits without any consistency. Our most consistent habits are usually our most harmful habits. We consistently watch TV at night. We consistently eat dessert after dinner, and the list goes on and on.

The other challenge with habits is that they are boring. Habits and routines quickly become dull and monotonous. I won't try to make them sound sexy and appealing because they aren't. This is why I believe English-American poet W.H. Auden's quote that "Routine in an intelligent man is a sign of ambition." It has to be a sign of ambition because there would be no other reason to stick to the monotonous tasks unless you were striving for something far greater in life.

In the beginning of this book, I told you I wanted it to be practical and useful to you. I don't care if you like this book and feel inspired if you don't end up getting results in the end. That would be a waste of your time in reading this and my time in writing it. If, at the end of the day, this book doesn't make you a better employee, boss, spouse, parent, or person, then I have failed massively. So in order to move toward those results, we must first evaluate our habits to see where we have consistency and discipline, and where we need improvement. Before we go on, take a minute to fill out the habits worksheet in Figure 2 on the next page. Think about this seriously. It could be a game changer for you if you allow it to be.

In the book *The One Thing*, authors Gary Keller and Jay Papasan cite research from the University College of London in 2009, which concluded that it took an average of sixty-six days to create a new habit. Unfortunately, most people don't last two weeks.

Jeff Young has some wise words about building habits, having overcome many obstacles himself. He was diagnosed with ALS (Lou Gehrig's Disease) in 1983 and was told he likely had three years to live. In 2018 Young is still coaching high school football and is a motivational writer! In one of his writings he said:

> Life, for the most part, is a series of habits. Bad habits are easily formed and most often simply fallen into. Good habits usually take conscious thought, consistency, and a lot of self-discipline to develop. Once you break the pattern of a good habit, how easy is it to slide back into old negative habits? And how tough is it to get back into your good habits once you've fallen out of them? If you are someone who struggles to maintain a diet or exercise schedule, you know exactly what I'm talking about.
>
> When you develop a set of habits, you steer your life in a direction that will eventually become your destiny. You will either consciously choose your destiny by getting hyper clear on exactly what you want in life and develop a set of habits that supports that destination, or you will most likely fall into a pattern of behavior that leaves you confused and frustrated about what you are doing, why you are doing it, and where life is taking you. This is not a place you want to end up. Once you have developed a set of habits that will put

What bad habits are you stuck in?

1. _____

2. _____

3. _____

What good habits are you doing consistently?

1. _____

2. _____

3. _____

What good habits could you start that would improve your life drastically?

1. _____

2. _____

3. _____

What bad habits *must* you break in order to have the life you desire?

1. _____

2. _____

3. _____

Figure 2: *Habits Worksheet*

you in alignment with the destiny you have decided must be yours, turn neither to the right nor to left. Keep in mind just how difficult it will be to recapture these good habits once you've let them go, and refuse to start the bad habit of not practicing a good habit. This is a habit you want nothing to do with.

One of my favorite parts of writing this book has been continually experiencing incredibly practical examples as I am writing. I just took a call that turned into a forty-five-minute conversation with a friend who feels lost and stuck in pursuing his dreams. It was difficult to do, but I firmly challenged him on his behaviors and habits I have seen over the years that are limiting his progress. In certain areas he is killing it, but there are a few key behaviors that boil down to a lack of consistency that are blocking him from his desired results.

Gary Vaynerchuk talks extensively about the importance of self-awareness and how rare it is to find people with it. The same was true for my friend until we had that honest and firm conversation. So I'm asking you right now: Can you handle taking an honest look in the mirror? Can you handle looking deep into your own heart and soul to see if you are truly living up to the values and behaviors you think and say are important? I know I am *not* in plenty of areas, and it drives me crazy that I am not always consistent with my values and standards. If this is the case for you as well, don't spend time wallowing in shame. Instead, make a small commitment to get better every day. Each act in the right direction makes a positive difference in the end no matter how small it is.

While writing about Aristotle's work, author, historian and philosopher Will Durant wrote, "We are what we repeatedly do. Excellence, then, is not an act but a habit." Look at that list you created and get real serious about it. Find a way to make those new habits a consistent reality in your life, and find a way to get rid of the bad ones once and for all. We will talk about tactics to help with this in the second half of the book.

In his book *The Compound Effect*, which I recommended earlier, Darren Hardy talks about how the little things are easy to do, but they are also just as easy not to do. This is the great challenge—inserting powerful habits that, over time, will have exponential impact on your life, finances, marriage, and health. This is very easy to do; unfortunately, it is also just as easy not to do, and that is what most people choose.

Our habits not only shape our results, but they also shape our character. That is a big deal, because our character is one of the most important things we carry in life. There is little I want more for my kids than for them to become men and women of character and to marry other men and women of character. Legendary UCLA basketball coach John Wooden once said, "Be more concerned with your character than your reputation, because character is what you really are, while your reputation is merely what others think you are."

Again, no one is going to notice overnight if you stop hitting the snooze button and start inserting small daily habits into your life. They may not notice for decades. But I assure you, in the end, you will notice and you will never regret it.

"Continuous effort—not strength or intelligence—is the key to unlocking our potential."

—Winston Churchill

Key Chapter Takeaways:

1. What if you didn't choose one or the other—consistency or intensity—but prioritized both? What would that do for your results? What would it do for your relationships? What would it do for your impact? I believe it would change everything for you!
2. As Jim Rohn discusses, we must all choose either the pain of discipline or the pain of regret. Discipline is the harder choice today, but it can prevent tremendous pain down the road.
3. The key to improving your life lies in your habitual routines and your consistent actions.

Living
Intentionally

"I never did anything worth doing by accident, nor did any of my inventions come by accident; they came by work."

—Plato

BEING INTENTIONAL IS A RARE SKILL in society today. With so many pressing demands and distractions all around us, we get swept up in the storm and rarely make time to sit down and think intentionally about who we want to be and what we really want to accomplish most. One of my primary goals is to help people be intentional about every aspect of their life and work. Too often we thrive in some areas while neglecting other areas completely. Often those neglected areas are even the ones that are most important to us.

The snooze button is a perfect example of intentionality. Each night we look at our schedule and workload the next day and make an *intentional* decision about what time we need to wake up to make it all happen. When we hit the snooze button on our alarm, we violate that thought-out decision we made the night before. This small violation of our intentions begins to seep into other areas of our lives and slowly erodes our self-confidence and identity. We are also in a more trustworthy state of thinking when we set our alarm than when it goes off and we want to hit snooze in our groggy morning daze.

Over the years through my work as a coach, I have found that living with intention is an incredibly rare practice. What a shame that is! We should all be intentional about the people we want to become and the dreams we want to achieve. Writer, director, and producer Jane Wagner once said, "All my life, I always wanted to be somebody. Now I see that I should have been more specific." Most success in life doesn't happen by accident. Once I realized that, it was a game changer for me. It is partially why I believe so much in receiving coaching. I realized that I needed accountability and support from others to either start being intentional in certain areas or maintain it in others.

We should all be intentional about the people we want to become and the dreams we want to achieve.

There are certain things that pretty much everyone wants. Most people who are married long for a passionate and thriving partnership. Most people want a fulfilling and meaningful career. Most parents want to be great at it and not make the same mistakes their parents made. Most people want to become their ideal self in all areas: fitness, relationships, leadership, finances, etc. However, wanting to become somebody and actually *being* that person are two completely different things. Based on my personal experience and in working with countless others, I am a firm believer that very few positive events will happen to us on accident. Most wonderful experiences don't just fall on our laps. Some do, but most won't. If you want to find your ideal mate, usually you first have to become someone worthy of attracting that type of person. And that takes intention!

When I was younger, I knew that one of my highest priorities in life was going to be striving to be an outstanding dad. It is one of the most important areas of life for me! I would rather toss all my other dreams of success and impact out the window and be an outstanding father if it came down to a choice between the two. Knowing how important that was to me, I started writing a letter to my future son when I was nineteen years old. I wanted to intentionally impart wisdom as I learned it, share life lessons and experiences, and give him a deeper glance into his father's personal growth and development as it occurred. I currently have forty-two pages typed to give to him when he turns eighteen. I'm sure it will be over a hundred pages by then. In that letter he will get to see everything from my deepest, darkest struggles to my highest highs.

He will read about my depression, the periods of life when I didn't want to live, as well as the moments when I was in love and was dating his future mom. He'll read my hopes and dreams, some of which have come true and others that never will. I hope

Lucy

Joshua

Andrew

it will be one of the best gifts he will ever receive. Unfortunately, I didn't think I would have a daughter first, or even think to start one for her for some foolish reason, so I started hers and my second son's once they were born and am playing catch-up.

Systems and Processes

Just wanting to be an outstanding father and deciding to start that letter would never have been enough to get me to over forty-two pages. I don't wake up on Tuesday morning and think, *In the midst of this crazy-busy day, maybe I should take some time and write in my letter to Josh*. If I relied on that, I would probably still be stuck somewhere below ten pages. I have a system that reminds me how often to write in his letter and makes sure I do. I strive to attach a system to most of my important intentions in life. If something matters enough to us, it is worth taking the time to prioritize it with systems and processes to ensure we live it out. I've got to say, this took a drastic re-shaping of my thinking to start implementing. By nature, I am more adventurous and carefree, but over time I realized that to live the fullest life with the most impact, I could benefit from implementing systems and processes to drive results. Don't get me wrong—systems don't fully replace spontaneity or passion. There are still plenty of times when I feel compelled to write in my kids' letters because they did something cute, we shared a poignant experience, or I just acquired some wisdom that I want to share. Systems add extra value, though, and drive a more consistent action and result.

It takes intention to create systems and processes. Intentionality is what truly separates the greats from the rest. It is what gives me confidence in someone else's dream. When I see they have mapped out an intentional plan and are working that plan, that is when I truly believe in someone. A few years ago, my younger brother, Will, had an opportunity to act in the movie *Wild* with Reese Witherspoon. This was a massive opportunity for my brother because his dream is to become an Academy Award–winning director. To encourage Will in his pursuit, in 2016, for his birthday, I got him a fake Oscar trophy

Birthday gift for my brother, Will.

with the inscription, *I promise!*

The reason I gave my brother this gift, and have this level of belief in him, is partially because of his incredible talent as a filmmaker at such a young age. However, it is not his natural talent that gives me the majority of my confidence in him. Talent, like ideas, is everywhere. The world is filled with incredibly talented people who fall short of their potential. My confidence is strongest because of his intentional focus on excellence, continuous improvement, and willingness to create a specific and mapped-out plan to intentionally pursue his goal. Three days after I gave my brother this trophy, he sent me the photo on the following page.

This is a photo of Will's strategic approach to winning his Oscar, with the year mapped out and everything. This is unique, this differentiates him, and this gives me confidence that one day I will be sitting in the audience watching my brother make his Oscar acceptance speech. Intentionality matters!

This is why intentionality is the great differentiator—because it determines your actions and behaviors. My brother takes on proj-

My brother's plan to achieve his goal.

ects, refines his skills, increases his knowledge, and connects with specific people strategically based on his end goal. His Oscar goal feeds into a bigger-picture goal as to the kind of director he wants to be and the levels of influence and impact he wants to achieve.

In life, we don't have to simply hop in the current, as so many do, and wait to see where the river will guide us. Intentionality is about a combination of embracing the river's flow while knowing when to put our paddle in and start maneuvering. At times we might even need to paddle upstream. Be willing to paddle upstream when necessary.

Coach Wooden was the master of intentionality. ESPN voted him the greatest coach in American sports history in 2009. His UCLA basketball team had an eighty-eight-game winning streak, a record in men's basketball that stands to this day. One of the characteristics that differentiated Wooden the most was his relentless intentional focus on constant, never-ending improvement. Each practice, Wooden wrote a detailed schedule, down to the minute, on three-by-five notecards. Then every summer he reviewed the cards to see how he could make his practices more effective and efficient the following year. It didn't work overnight. He coached fifteen seasons at UCLA without winning a single championship. All of a sudden, though, the work and intentional focus started to pay off, and his team won ten out of the next twelve national championships—another record that still stands to this day!

Living intentionally is not simply about our planning and our actions. Living intentionally also affects our values and character. When we don't do it well, it creates what I call the Values Gap.

The Values Gap

I believe that one of the biggest internal struggles most of us have comes as a result of a gap in our values. I define the Values Gap as the distance between the person we believe we should be and the person we consistently are. Everyone's gap is a different size, and the size of our gap affects our lives in significant ways.

Average Person's Gap
Real Self--Ideal Self

Outstanding Person's Gap
Real Self-------Ideal Self

The larger the gap, the more intense our struggle with self-worth and self-efficacy is likely to be. The larger the gap, the more we create a negative identity for ourselves that tends to be picked up by other people as well, which also limits our potential. Many times this gap is the number one factor preventing people from achieving their dreams and desires. It takes a high level of intentionality to close this gap. My older brother, Chris, taught me to ask a question that exposes this gap in daily situations: "How would my ideal self act in this situation?" It is amazing how clear the answer usually is and can lead us to powerful and intentional actions. I can't tell you how many times this question has saved me from making a stupid decision and changed my behavior completely. It is probably the most powerful question I have learned to ask myself on a consistent basis.

The first step to closing the Values Gap is awareness. Creating awareness takes intentionality. If you can intentionally attack your Values Gap and start closing it, you will see incredibly powerful shifts in your life. Most people simply drift through life. Intentionality is what truly separates the greats from the rest.

"I am here for purpose and that purpose is to grow into a mountain, not to shrink to a grain of sand. Henceforth will I apply all my efforts to become the highest mountain of all and I will strain my potential until it cries for mercy."

—Og Mandino

Key Chapter Takeaways:

1. Very few positive events will happen to us on accident. Real and consistent results require intentional effort.
2. Intentionality is what truly separates the greats from the rest. Living an intentional life is a rare and beautiful sight in today's society.
3. We don't have to simply hop in the current, as so many do, and wait to see where the river will guide us. Intentionality is about a combination of embracing the river's flow while knowing when to put our paddle in and start maneuvering. At times we might even need to paddle upstream. Be willing to paddle upstream when necessary.

Interest vs. Commitment

"Commitment is what transforms a promise into reality. It is the words that speak boldly of your intentions. And the actions which speak louder than the words."

—Abraham Lincoln

SO OFTEN WE THINK interest is enough, but I can promise you that it almost never is. Interest doesn't change the world; commitment does. Interest doesn't improve your marriage; commitment does. Interest doesn't help you break through in your career, but relentless commitment does. Interest is setting your alarm the night before. Commitment is not hitting the snooze button the next morning when the alarm goes off. Darren Hardy says, "Commitment is doing the thing you said you were going to do long after the mood you said it in has left you." That is the difference between interest and commitment.

Essentialism

Commitment requires knowing your priorities deeply and being able to discern what is truly essential versus everything else. In his book *Essentialism*, author Greg McKeown describes the basic value proposition of essentialism. He says, "Only once you give yourself permission to stop trying to do it all. To stop saying yes to everyone, can you make your highest contribution towards the things that really matter." This is very difficult to do in the 21st century. With countless opportunities at every turn, it's challenging to stick to what matters most to us. Often we bounce back and forth from one interest to another, don't become masters at a skill or trade, and have minimal impact in every space we operate in. I have heard that a powerful *yes* must be defended by 1,000 *no's*. Life is a series of tradeoffs, and commitment requires saying *no* to many *good* opportunities so you can say *yes* to the *great* ones.

> *Interest is setting your alarm the night before. Commitment is not hitting the snooze button the next morning when the alarm goes off.*

Commitment Requires Time

Swedish psychologist Anders Ericsson came up with the 10,000-hour rule, which Malcolm Gladwell made famous in his book *Outliers*. Ericsson wrote about the 10,000-hour rule in a 1993 paper called "The Role of Deliberate Practice in the Acquisition of Expert Performance." Essentially, Ericsson highlighted research that demonstrated how most of society has traditionally thought about talent is wrong. Instead of natural talent being the primary differentiator between the elite performers and the rest of us, the research shows that the peak performers typically acquired over 10,000 hours of deliberate practice in their given field. He stated that "many character-istics once believed to reflect innate talent are actually the result of intense practice extended for a minimum of 10 years." Unfortunate-ly, the research eliminates the full validity of our continual excuses that the people who are outperforming us were simply born better. While natural talent of course plays a role in our potential and limi-tations, it typically plays a much less significant role than most of us would like to admit. Intentional focus and commitment actually play the larger role. Most of us need to stop dabbling and start commit-ting by playing full out in our fields of passion and areas that matter most to us.

When five other Oregon State students and I started our non-profit, Ncompass, over a decade ago, we had some big dreams! I thought that by our fifth year as an organization, we would be rais-ing millions of dollars a year to empower youth all around the world. However, it wasn't until nearly the end of our tenth year that we raised our cumulative millionth dollar. If this was something we were just interested in, not committed to, then we would have quit a long time ago because it is a heck of a lot harder than we ever thought it was going to be when we started the organization as college students. However, because of our commitment and patience, we raised more money in our tenth year than we did in our first seven years com-bined! And now we are finally starting to experience the compound effect in an exciting way, sending over 130 kids in Haiti to school, and supporting dozens of other kids through mentoring, housing, and medical care among other services. Interest doesn't change the world; commitment does!

Success for Impact

My hope for this book is not that it helps you be successful for the sake of self. My goal is that you learn tools and tactics to help you achieve success for the sake of impact. That you live a life worthy of your potential and impact this world in a special way that only you can. No one else has the same story as you. No one else has the same

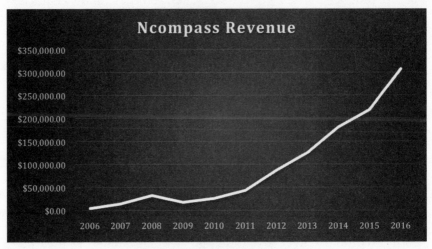

Ncompass Historical Revenue

Our incredible kids in Titanyen, Haiti.

combination of skills and passions as you. When you combine all of it together, you can leave your imprint in this world as unique as the fingerprint you carry. None of this happens though, until interest is transformed to commitment. I have heard the quote attributed to author Ken Blanchard that summarizes this chapter well. "There's a difference between interest and commitment. When you're interested in doing something, you do it only when it's convenient. When you are committed to something, you accept no excuses, only results." What are you committed to in life? What areas of life will you reject your excuses and accept only results? The world needs your commitment now more than ever.

"A man should conceive of a legitimate purpose in his heart, and set out to accomplish it.... He should make this purpose his supreme duty, and should devote himself to its attainment, not allowing his thoughts to wander away into ephemeral fancies, longings, and imaginings. This is the royal road to self-control and true concentration of thought."

—James Allen

Key Chapter Takeaways:

1. Interest doesn't change the world; commitment does.
2. While natural talent of course plays a role in our potential and limitations, it typically plays a much less significant role than most of us would like to admit. Research shows that intentional focus and commitment actually play the larger role.
3. No one else has the same story as you. No one else has the same combination of skills and passions as you. When you combine all of it together, you can leave an imprint in this world as unique as the fingerprint you carry.

7

All In

"*When you do the common things of life in an uncommon way, you will command the attention of the world.*"

—George Washington Carver

IT IS SO EVIDENT that doing the common things in an uncommon way is a rare treasure in today's world. The companies and individuals who understand this usually rise to the top fairly quickly because of how rare it is.

We live in an era marked by low quality, low commitment, and total satisfaction with mediocrity and the status quo. There aren't many people or organizations who challenge us to be more, do more, and give more. We are rarely challenged to give our absolute best and play full out in all we do.

De-Seed the Lemon

Recently at a conference, I was blessed to hear global leadership advisor and author Robin Sharma speak. He talked about the importance of excellence and drove the point home through an example

51

of a recent train ride he'd taken. He asked the server for water with lemons on the side. He said when the lemon wedges were brought out, he noticed instantly that this was an organization dedicated to excellence. What he noticed was that they had de-seeded the lemons. They simply removed the seeds. It probably didn't take them more than a few seconds, but he noticed it. This small act was the inches that made the difference between typical and excellent. De-seed the lemon! Make this a consistent practice and philosophy in all you do!

Strive to under-promise and over-deliver. We live in a culture that constantly over-promises and under-delivers. Flip the equation!

Author and motivational speaker Zig Ziglar said it best: "The elevator to success is out of service. But the stairs are always open." Excellence requires taking the stairs every day, week, month, and year. It requires striving to figure out what details and inches make the difference between good and great, and then taking action.

What do you have to do to add more value and differentiate yourself in everything you do? Think about this seriously. I once worked with a guy named Dave Campbell who said, "You've got to puke blood before you achieve excellence." Excellence has a price, and you need to look it square in the eye and either accept it or reject it. As I write this section, it is 12:10 a.m. on a Saturday night. I am tired and ready to go to bed, but I have at least another hour or two of writing because I am committed to producing the best book I am capable of and getting it on the market as quickly as possible. You have to look excellence in the eyes, confront the level of sacrifice it will require of you, and make your decision and commitment. Apple cofounder Steve Jobs consistently made similar decisions and commitments to excellence.

Dream Big. Act Small.

If you have studied Jobs at all, you know that he was a man with massive dreams and aspirations. He tried to convince us to "put a dent in the universe" and that "the people who are crazy enough to think they can change the world are the ones who do." However, I believe the greatest legacy Jobs left Apple was not his grandiose thinking, but his insane attention and focus on excellence and small details. In my TEDx talk titled "Dream Big. Act Small," I point out that if you have an iPhone and use your flashlight icon, you will notice that when you turn it on, a small switch flips up, just like the one on a real flashlight. At the time of this writing, most other phones neglect this small and seemingly insignificant detail. And while most of you never noticed this before, and this one small detail is not why Apple is considered to be so successful, I do believe it plays a major role in their success. Apple's effort to put excellence into tiny details like this over years and decades is why the company is worth over $900 billion today and is one of the most valuable companies in the world.

Being vs. Doing

I have heard the quote attributed to Doug Firebaugh, "Achievement to most people is something you do...to the high achiever, it is something you are." At first, excellence emerges through actions and behavior, but eventually it transforms into your identity and your character. Sometimes we simply have to start *doing*, before it eventually turns into *being*. I urge you to start now! Make a commitment to start living *all in*, and adding value by delivering on a whole different level. Make the commitment so strong and rewire your standards so effectively that everyone around you will notice it without you having to say a word. What and who we become starts with an initial decision and commitment. Make that commitment now!

Think about the majority of people in society and how they operate. Many people have low or no standards. Way too many people don't like their jobs or are planning on leaving their jobs in the next few months, so they give poor effort. Instead of doing that, I urge you to adopt the mindset: *How I do one thing is how I do everything*, and give your best effort wherever you are right now. Carol Dweck, psychology professor at Stanford University and author of the book *Mindset*, says, "Effort is one of those things that gives meaning to life. Effort means you care about something, that something is important to you and you are willing to work for it."

The last person I ever want to hire is the person who gave poor to moderate effort in their last job but is going to try to convince me that they just weren't passionate about that job, and since this is really what they want to do, they are going to be awesome now. I per-

What and who we become starts with an initial decision and commitment.

sonally don't buy it. I think we wire ourselves with a certain standard and that standard carries over to other areas of our lives. If you come watch me play flag football, you'll notice that I dive for any ball I have a chance at even touching with my fingertips. I will break myself to try to catch a ball that is probably out of reach anyway on the chance that I might surpass my own expectations and those of others around me. That same spirit, passion, and commitment are what I strive to bring to the table for anything I engage in.

Am I perfect? Is everything I do excellent? No! Not even close. But you can sure bet that I give all I have to all I do. I pour my heart and soul into it, and I am always striving to make it better. I am fully committed to constant, never-ending improvement. I will never arrive or feel like I have made it in any area. I can always be a better coach for my clients, husband for my wife, father to my kids, and leader to my people. Always! And so can you! We all have another level inside of us. Let's work together to tap into it.

Quality

Henry Ford said, "Quality means doing it right when no one is looking." That is how you differentiate yourself. How many people do quality work when someone is watching? Almost everyone. But how many people do it while no one is watching? Almost no one.

I love this photo:

THE DISTANCE
BETWEEN
WINNING &
LOSING

You never know when someone is watching.

The photo above shows an athlete who thought no one was watching, so he didn't go *all in* and make the effort for peak performance. We have to convince ourselves that someone is always watching. Whatever you have to do in order to do that, do it! The snooze button is one of those areas where no one is watching. It is in the comfort of your bedroom behind closed doors that you decide whether you'll hit the snooze button or not. Make the decision to be *all in*, even when no one is watching.

"Champions are champions not because they do anything extraordinary but because they do the ordinary things better than anyone else."

—Chuck Noll

Key Chapter Takeaways:

1. Doing the common things in an uncommon way is a rare treasure in today's world. Never underestimate the power of doing small things with great focus and deliberate care.
2. We live in a culture that constantly over-promises and under-delivers. Flip the equation! Be someone who always delivers more value than you say you will, and the world will take notice.
3. If you want to stand out amongst the masses, you need to put in an immense amount of effort when no one is watching. If you do that for years and decades, eventually the world will take notice.

PART TWO

Taking Action

Start Now

"*Three things you never get back—time, words, and opportunity.*"

—Anonymous

I RECENTLY ATTENDED Brendon Burchard's High Performance Academy in San Diego. One of the most powerful ideas I received from his intense, four-day conference was this concept he kept driving home: "Start clunky!" In college I used to have a poster hanging in my room of a little boy learning to swim with the quote "Everything is difficult before it is easy." I tell my kids this often. When we are just starting something, we usually aren't very good. Often we allow this to prevent us from being vulnerable enough to even *start*. When I came back from that conference, I decided I was going to begin writing my books and start making more videos for my business. I am not naturally a very good writer (you may agree!), and I hated making videos, but I also knew that in order to drive the impact I wanted to create in this world, I would need to become better at both. The only way to do that is to start! This book is a result of Brendon Burchard's encouragement to "start clunky." My videos are slowly getting better, and I can tell that even my writing is improving as well. Nothing becomes easy overnight, though. It takes time! Most skills and behaviors take years before they become easy.

In their book *Do Hard Things*, twin brothers Alex and Brett Harris encourage us with the words: "Anything worth doing is worth doing poorly—at first." I love this quote! At first glance, it seems counter to everything I talked about in the previous chapter on excellence, but I believe they are simply expressing the truth that when you try something new, you are likely not going to be very good. You still strive for excellence and give *your* best in that moment, but in order to become good, you have to be willing to fail, which means being willing to start.

Sometimes I think it is simply a feeling of overwhelm that prevents us from doing the little things and moving in the direction we desire. Don't let overwhelm win! So often we look around us and feel like the pain, suffering, and problems around us are too big and we can't make a difference, but

> *In order to become good, you have to be willing to fail, which means being willing to start.*

as Mother Teresa once said, "If you can't feed one hundred people, then just feed one." When she wanted to start her work in Calcutta, she was asked what she must do to consider the work successful. "I do not know what success will be," she replied, "but if the Missionaries of Charity have brought joy to one unhappy home—made one innocent child from the street keep pure for Jesus—one dying person die in peace with God—don't you think...it would be worthwhile offering everything for just that one?"

I wish more people believed and acted this way. No, you can't prevent all the deaths of the thousands of people who die each day of hunger-related causes or educate all the millions of kids around the world without access to education. But you can help one of them, or maybe two or ten. Don't let overwhelm in helping others or in what it will take to achieve your dreams prevent you from taking action today. Just focus on one day at a time. One action at a time.

Someday Never Happens for Most People

During spring break of my sophomore year in college, one of my best friends, Andy, and I started talking about how much suffering there was in the world, and how someday we should start a nonprofit to do something about it. A few years later, during our final year of college, he came to me one day and said, "Someday never happens for most people. Let's just start this thing today and see where it goes." At first I was apprehensive and a little afraid. Like so many other people, I felt unprepared, unqualified, and not ready to take on such a large undertaking. But something about Andy's boldness and the sheer truth in his statement that "Someday never happens for most people" gave me the courage to take the leap with him and three other friends we then recruited. Taking that leap was one of the best decisions I have ever made and has provided me with some of my deepest friendships, most magical experiences, and the most meaningful work in my life. There are dozens of kids in Haiti who I love dearly today as a result of Andy's willingness to *start* before we were ready.

Don't get me wrong, we have made countless mistakes along the way as a result of our inexperience and youth in those early days. It has been way harder than I ever thought it would be, and I definitely don't recommend that everyone start their own nonprofit, especially not while in college. However, for some people, starting now is exactly what you need to do in some specific area of life. Maybe you're not meant to start a nonprofit today, but just need to write your first check to a charity that stirs your heart. Or maybe you could finally sign up to mentor that kid you have been thinking about. Whatever it is you feel called to do that you have been putting off, find the courage and boldness to start. Don't wait for life to pass you by. It will go much quicker than any of us think.

In 2004, as Andy and I were having that first conversation about the potential of starting our nonprofit, three thousand miles away in Haiti, a man named Jackson Ismorin was making his own bold decision to start before he was ready. At the young age of twenty-four, Jackson took in twenty-five kids off the streets after severe flooding left a large number of them without parents. He then faithfully cared for and supported those kids until we met in 2007 and partnered with him in the mission he had been so faithfully stewarding. Jackson spent the rest of his young life caring for the children with everything he had to give, until at the age of thirty-two he died in a tragic car accident.

Jackson's death was devastating to our nonprofit and to the kids in Haiti. But the legacy that Jackson left through his courage and willingness to start before he felt ready has left dozens of kids in a better position today than they ever thought possible. Now, new

My dear friend, Jackson Ismorin.

committed leaders have stepped in, filled Jackson's shoes, and carry his legacy on through their dedicated service and sacrifice.

Imagine if Jackson had never started the orphanage or if Mother Teresa never started the Missionaries of Charity. Imagine if Mahatma Gandhi never started his nonviolent protests in India or if Martin Luther King Jr. never had a dream. Imagine if you never_____.

"Start where you are. Use what you have. Do what you can."

—Arthur Ashe

Key Chapter Takeaways:

1. In order to become good, you have to be willing to fail, which means being willing to start. Take Brendon Burchard's advice and "Start clunky!"
2. Someday never happens for most people.
3. Don't wait to start making an impact in the world until you have more wisdom, more money, or more time. Give what you have with where you are at right now. The world needs you now more than ever.

9

The Peak Performance Cycle

"Productivity is never an accident. It is always the result of a commitment to excellence, intelligent planning, and focused effort."

—Paul J. Meyer

WHEN YOU ARE TRYING to accomplish anything, whether it is avoiding the snooze button, losing thirty pounds, or running a successful company, it is always good to evaluate the benchmarks and stories of other people or related organizations who have been successful. If you are striving to achieve peak performance at the highest levels, who better to study than Olympic gold medalists?

One such peak performer changed my life forever when I was nineteen years old. At this point in my life, I had probably only read about three books from cover to cover. That's right, parents and teachers, I used CliffsNotes and skimmed my way through school (but would give anything to go back and do it differently!). It wasn't until my freshman year of college, when I picked up the book *Slaying the Dragon* by Michael Johnson, that my love for reading was born! Johnson won four Olympic gold medals and set the world record for the 200-meter and 400-meter races in the 1990s. In his book, Johnson talks about his childhood and how his father stressed the importance of goal setting and mapping out a life plan. When he presented his dreams as a child, his father didn't just encourage him—he also asked him what his plan was to achieve them. He challenged his son, even as a child, to always have a strategy to achieve what he wanted in life.

Since reading his book, I have been relentless in setting yearly and monthly goals. He taught me a process of achievement that I have been using ever since. I recently created a simplified model

PEAK PERFORMANCE CYCLE

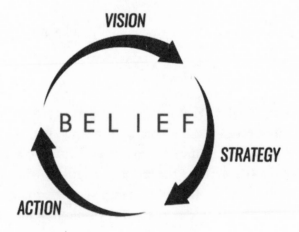

Figure 3: *The Peak Performance Cycle*

called the Peak Performance Cycle, a three-step process highlighting four primary categories where peak performers thrive.

"Vision without action is merely a dream. Action without vision just passes the time. Vision with action can change the world."

—Joel A. Barker

Sustained peak performance requires a clear vision, an aligned strategy, consistent action, and relentless belief. Think about how Olympians exemplify the Peak Performance Cycle. Their *vision* has no ambiguity. For example: become the fastest person on earth to run the 200-meter dash. It's hard to get any clearer than that. Then they hire coaches to help them set their training *strategy* and constantly modify it to ensure they are maximizing every opportunity and hour of preparation. They have strategies for their nutrition, fitness, injury prevention, and practice time. Then these top-level athletes do what most of us fail to do on a daily basis—they put the plan into *action*! Lastly, they maintain a relentless *belief* that they're capable of achieving it. Belief is right at the heart of the Peak Performance Cycle, yet one of its most underestimated factors. Belief is the fuel for action! I will cover this topic more in chapter 13.

Sustained peak performance requires a clear vision, an aligned strategy, consistent action, and relentless belief.

It's not just Olympic athletes who model this cycle. You can find this consistent practice from high-performing CEOs, managers, teachers, parents, coaches, and more. If you see greatness around you in any area of life, the Peak Performance Cycle is probably somewhere nearby.

If mastered, I believe this method will improve literally every area of your life. Over the next few chapters, we'll talk about how vision, strategy, action, and belief can relate to the snooze button and change other key habits in your life.

"Worthwhile results come from hard work and careful planning."

—John Wooden

Key Chapter Takeaways:

1. Sustained peak performance requires a clear vision, an aligned strategy, consistent action, and relentless belief.
2. Every dream needs a concrete and actionable plan to make it a likely reality.
3. The Peak Performance Cycle can be used to improve any area of your life. Pick an area and test the process to see if you can take your results to another level.

10

Clear Vision

"*The two most important days in your life are the day you are born and the day you find out why.*"

—Attributed to Mark Twain

MOST OF US LACK a clear and compelling vision that gives us the motivation to get up early and stay up late when necessary. It is the clear and compelling goal that Olympic athletes have, which gives them the discipline to avoid the excess chocolate, alcohol, and TV time, that so many of us constantly battle with (and usually lose).

Establishing a clear vision is easier said than done though. Just like any other area of life, everyone is looking for the one-step formula to achieve it. Most people are unwilling to do the mental heavy lifting it takes to truly find it. We are simply undisciplined in our thoughts. Bringing clarity to the vision you have for your business, marriage, health, or any other category of life takes time and energy, both of which are always in short supply.

Retreat and Reflect

When was the last time you went on a backpacking trip alone? Attended a silent retreat? Turned off your phone for an entire day? I'm guessing you can't remember. Our fast-paced world doesn't allow for this kind of time for reflection unless you fight for it.

I am just as guilty as most in this area. I desperately long for those moments without distraction. I think one of the most brilliant commercials ever is the one in which people in an SUV are driving around looking for cell phone service, continually going from one location to another. In the end, the commercial reveals they were actually looking for a spot without service to get away from all the distractions. Lately I have been putting my phone on airplane mode for hours at a time during the day so I can focus on key tasks and avoid getting distracting texts and calls. I started this habit after reading the book *The One Thing* I cited earlier in which authors Kellar and Papasan challenge us to work with the same levels of focus we expect pilots and surgeons to use. We would all probably be quite frustrated if our surgeon was texting his friends midway through operating on our knee. This challenge has helped me accomplish more work in less time, while staying focused on the original goal and vision I started my day with.

One of my favorite vacations ever was a trip to Mazatlán with my wife a few years ago. Our cell phones had no service, and it was so refreshing to our souls! It took about forty-eight hours of checking our pockets, expecting to have messages or needing to respond to supposed "urgent" requests before we realized we could disconnect and let go! Inevitably, my dreaming started to increase, and my creativity started to expand. Our excitement and vision for our marriage improved as well, and we saw new possibilities for the next year of our lives.

Clarity is Power

John Maxwell says, "You must know your dream before you can attract your team." When your vision is clear, it has the power to start drawing the right people to you to help make it a reality. If you don't need a dream team to pull off your vision, then you aren't dreaming big enough.

Writer and radio personality Earl Nightingale once said, "People with goals succeed because they know where they're going." How can you expect to have a thriving marriage if you haven't defined what that looks like for you? What if it looks different to you than it does to your spouse and you have never discussed it? A business consulting group came and spoke to our MBA program at OSU once, and one of the speakers said, "Unspoken expectations are disappointments waiting to happen." I have never forgotten that concept and have experienced its truth many times over the years.

One of my first serious conversations with my wife, Stephanie, revealed to me that she had a clear vision of what she wanted from a husband. He was home most nights of the week and had weekends off. I, on the other hand, had spent the last three years thinking I was never going to get married or have kids following Kate's death in the car accident. My vision prior to dating Stephanie was to work forty hours a week in a business career and run the nonprofit for another forty hours each week—not your ideal family work-life balance. But we sat outside my apartment in downtown Portland talking openly and honestly about our expectations. I told her I wanted to be there for my family and never be a neglectful father, but I also had a mission I was passionate about and committed to that would take a great deal of time, energy, and effort. I told her I was not the guy who would be home at five o'clock every night and consistently have weekends off. We both confronted the brutal facts, and together we decided that we could both come to a happy middle ground. This would always be an area of challenge with mild tension in our marriage, and it still is, but because we both understand each other's desires and are fully committed to *us*, our family, and our mission, we can and will make it work. All it took was open conversation and a search for clarity to gain this level of understanding and honesty.

Start with Why

Author Simon Sinek delivered a phenomenal TED Talk titled "How Great Leaders Inspire Action." This is now the third most-watched TED Talk of all time with over 38 million views. In his talk, he walks through the importance of starting with *why*, which is also the premise and title of his book, *Start with Why*. Sinek shows us that the truly great companies like Apple and the transformative leaders like Martin Luther King Jr. all communicated from their purpose first. They clearly articulated their reasons for why they were in business or leading movements both with themselves and with others. This is why they were so effective and left such a powerful impact on society. As Jack Welch, former CEO of General Electric says, "Good business leaders create a vision, articulate the vision, passionately own the vision, and relentlessly drive it to completion." It all starts with a clear and compelling vision.

In order to speak to others about your purpose and vision effectively, you have to fully understand it yourself. In his book *The Practice of Management*, Peter Drucker retells a favorite story about three stonecutters who were asked what they were doing. "The first replied: 'I am making a living.' The second kept on hammering while he said: 'I am doing the best job of stone cutting in the entire country.' The third one looked up with a visionary gleam in his eyes and said: 'I am building a cathedral.'"

In order to speak to others about your purpose and vision effectively, you have to fully understand it yourself.

If you want to achieve any goal, you need a strong *why* behind it. The *why* is where the juice comes from. It is your purpose that will carry you over the obstacles that are bound to come your way. It is the purpose that will give you the motivation to get up to your alarm the first time every morning when everything in you is begging you to hit snooze and stay in bed!

If you bought this book hoping to stop hitting the snooze button, your *why* probably needs to be stronger. If, for example, you have wanted to lose weight for years and haven't achieved it yet, your *why* probably isn't strong enough. In other words, you haven't figured out how to tap into it deeply or often enough to create the leverage necessary for change. Be patient, as specific strategies and ideas are coming in a few short chapters to help you achieve this!

"Your vision will become clear only when you look into your heart. Who looks outside, dreams. Who looks inside awakens."

—Carl Jung

Key Chapter Takeaways:

1. The journey ahead is filled with so many obstacles that in order to be successful, you need to have a clear vision with a compelling purpose.
2. Our fast-paced world doesn't allow for time for reflection unless you fight for it. In order to identify and maintain a clear and compelling vision, you must prioritize time away to reflect and seek clarity.
3. If you want to achieve any goal, you need a strong *why* behind it. The *why* is where the juice comes from. It is your purpose that will carry you over the obstacles that are bound to come your way.

Aligned Strategy

"Our goals can only be reached through a vehicle of a plan, in which we must fervently believe, and upon which we must vigorously act. There is no other route to success."

—Pablo Picasso

HAVING A CLEAR VISION is great and all, and you can have the best plan for your life typed on gold-plated paper, but with the wrong strategy, it won't do you much good. Consider the writer who wants to become a world-renowned author, and decides to read three books a week and write only two hours a month. That strategy will obviously never lead them to accomplish their vision. A clear vision without an effective strategy just doesn't work!

Outside Input

This is why many elite performers in a variety of fields around the world have coaches and there has been an explosion in the coaching industry. People are starting to understand the benefits of coaching and how it can apply to all areas of their lives. CEOs have executive coaches, many couples have hired marriage coaches (my wife and me included), athletes have fitness coaches, and people hire trainers and nutritionists. Coaches help in several key areas:

1. They often bring knowledge or expertise in a field you need assistance in.
2. They help you clarify your goals, dreams, and visions for the future.
3. They provide strategic refinement and necessary adaptation.
4. They provide consistent accountability.
5. They celebrate your successes and milestones.

Quick conflict-of-interest confession: I am a coach by trade and therefore quite biased in my belief in the value of coaching. However, I also put my money and time where my mouth is. I have hired a Tony Robbins certified coach, consulted a SCORE business coach, and hired marriage coaches. I also send weekly scorecards (which I'll describe in chapter 14) to coaches of mine in marketing, business, and my personal life to help me measure and track key behaviors. I have found there is a powerful element to having someone looking in from the outside. It helps reveal our inherent biases. Whether you are a company or an individual, it is always good to have outside support and someone who challenges you to be your best. Ultimately, every decision has to be decided from the inside, but you should also have key input from the outside. Just another set of eyes and ears is powerful. This is why Ncompass has an advisory board and why I have coaches and mentors.

Tony Robbins said, "It's in your moments of decision that your destiny is shaped." Strategy is all about decision—which direction to move, when to move there, and how to move there most effectively and efficiently. Decisions are powerful. Hopefully as you read this book, you are making many critical decisions to take your life to the next level.

Focus

After many years of coaching and consulting, I've come to believe that one of the primary prohibiting factors of success is a lack of strategic focus. Yes, laziness is a factor for some, but it's not solely a lack of effort that causes most of us to falter—it's usually shallow thinking. Many of us are unwilling or unskilled in thinking strategically with deep focus. In our fast-paced, whirlwind society, it is becoming more and more difficult to make time for focused strategic thinking.

I have coached many young people in the past, often focusing on selecting the right university, proper major, post-college career track, or first job. Most of the time, I find they have barely thought about these critical life decisions. They have almost never thoroughly researched the university or its majors. They usually have not talked to their mentors and role models to help them through the process, and haven't shadowed someone who works in their prospective career field to see if they are actually interested in that type of work. They typically haven't interviewed anyone to ask about the average pay and common workplace culture. To be fair, I wasn't any different at their age.

This is often true of the older generations as well. People have goals and dreams they just hope will happen without having any semblance of a plan. We can't hope our way into success and accomplishment. "Hope is not a strategy," advises Rick Page in his book of the same title. You need a clearly defined, focused, and disciplined strategy.

Pastor Harry Emerson Fosdick said, "No life ever grows great until it is focused, dedicated, and disciplined." Many people aren't crushing it in their careers because their strategy and *focus* aren't refined, and they don't slow down long enough to properly align themselves for success. When most people fail, it's because they aren't strategically focused. They drift from one project to another, delivering mediocre results in all their work.

Time management practices are no longer enough. In today's

fast-paced world we are in desperate need of focus management. You can study efficiency all you want and add all sorts of tools and systems to manage your life better, but until you learn to refine and narrow your focus, you will struggle to make progress and gain momentum. Tim Ferriss, author of *The 4-Hour Workweek*, puts it this way: "Being busy is a form of laziness—lazy thinking."

Your strategy is the pathway you walk toward your ultimate goal. So many people have a dream that means everything to them, but they never even step on the path that leads to their desired destination. This is way too common! We have millions of people all around the country whose strategic actions don't align at all with where they are hoping to be five years from now.

If you *really* want your dream, then take the time to constantly refine, reshape, and transform your strategy! It takes disciplined thought, not just disciplined action. Don't waste too much time walking down the wrong path in the wrong direction. My good friend Kris Asleson, a nonprofit founder and director, entrepreneur, and husband, said to me, "If I don't have peace about where I am going, I don't want to be going there very fast." This is a great point, and life is too short to move slowly, so instead of doing that for too long, make a commitment to spend the necessary time aligning a strategy with your vision so that your time walking the path will be effective.

Your strategy is the pathway you walk toward your ultimate goal.

Setting your alarm the night before is all about effective planning. Knowing exactly what time you need to get up to make the most of your day is critical to your success. If you are struggling to stop hitting the snooze button, you probably need a new strategy. Placing your phone across the room so you have to get out of bed is a strategy. Downloading the app Mathe Alarm Clock that makes you solve an equation before you can turn off your alarm is a strategy. I will cover other tools and tactics in chapter 14.

Taking the time to prepare is being strategic. It helps you not just work harder but also work smarter than your competition. Start spending adequate time preparing for the task and challenge at hand. Don't neglect the planning process.

Adapt and Adjust

Even when you plan and prepare well, failure will still cross your path. When this occurs, heed John Maxwell's wise words: "Failed plans should not be interpreted as a failed vision. Visions don't change, they are only refined. Plans rarely stay the same, and are scrapped or adjusted as needed. Be stubborn about the vision, but flexible with your plan." Your plans will fail often and will need perpetual adjustment. I am altering my strategy constantly. Stick with a strategy long enough to ensure it has a chance to prove itself, but be quick to change it when you realize it won't produce the desired effect or lead you to your goal. Take it from two wise men: Confucius, a Chinese philosopher, said, "When it is obvious that the goals cannot be reached, don't adjust the goals, adjust the action steps." Zig Ziglar said, "When obstacles arise, you change your direction to reach your goal, you do not change your decision to get there."

"There is always a way to do it better...find it."

—Thomas Edison

Key Chapter Takeaways:

1. If you *really* want your dream, then take the time to constantly refine, reshape, and transform your strategy! It takes disciplined thought, not just disciplined action.

2. Stick with a strategy long enough to ensure it has a chance to prove itself, but be quick to change it when you realize it won't produce the desired effect or lead you to your goal.

3. You can study efficiency all you want and add all sorts of tools and systems to manage your life better, but until you learn to refine and narrow your focus, you will struggle to make progress and gain momentum.

Consistent Action

"Vision is the blueprint, belief is the foundation, but only hard work and a can do spirit can make it happen."

—R. E. Shockley

SOME OF YOUR PLANS are going to get derailed. You will get knocked down; it happens to all the greats and is part of the journey! Use it, learn from it, and grow through it. As champion boxer Mike Tyson said, "Everyone has a plan until they get punched in the mouth." When you inevitably take those hits, you simply have to step back, reevaluate, and decide whether to keep going or to create a new plan and move on.

As vision without strategy is ultimately ineffective, vision and strategy by themselves are massively incomplete. It isn't until you go to that final step, put the rubber to the road, and start taking consistent action, that things really start to move. As clergyman Henry Van Dyke said, "Some succeed because they are destined to, but most succeed because they are determined to." Don't kid yourself and think you can coast on your talents. Having a great vision and a well-thought-out plan doesn't mean you will be a guaranteed success. Every business leader knows that *execution is everything!*

Ideas are a dime a dozen; and many people get very excited about them. We are surrounded by stories of grandeur in Elon Musk, Steve Jobs, Mark Zuckerberg, and Bill Gates. We often think the reason they hit it big was because of their big idea, forgetting that it was actually their ability to execute on the idea that made all the difference. Think of Facebook vs. Myspace. We see it in case after case—the idea in and of itself doesn't work without a leader and team capable of executing.

I have *big* ideas every year, many of which I think could be billion-dollar businesses. Most of the time, ideas are all they are, though, because they're ideas I know I don't have the time, talent, or resources to execute on yet. I don't think I am special for having the ideas. I am only special if I am the guy who can pull them off. This is true for everyone.

Stop waiting around to join the countless masses of people claiming they had that great idea before it ever happened. No one cares and neither should you. Focus on what you can actually pull off, and make it happen!

Action Is the Great Differentiator!

Action is what separates the people who make it to the top and the countless souls scattered along the path bloodied and beaten down by the challenges of life. Starting isn't always easy, which is why I devoted a whole chapter to it earlier. However, starting is just the beginning and must be followed by dedicated and consistent action.

I recently met with an international speaker and asked him what separated him from so many other people who tried walking the same path but failed. His answer: He kept acting long after his competition quit. He was willing to lose everything to pursue his calling, and no obstacle would halt his consistent action in the direction of his dreams.

Tony Robbins said, "What changes your life is NOT learning

more. What changes your life is making decisions and using your personal power and taking action." Alan Fine, founder of Inside-Out Development, adds to that concept with his powerful quote, "If knowledge really were all it took...we'd all be incredible managers, great teachers, phenomenal parents and performers. But obviously we're not. Why? Because typically, the biggest obstacle to great performance isn't not knowing what to do; it's doing what we know." I love how he puts it!

We have access to more knowledge today than at any point in human history. Even many materially poor people around the world have access to unlimited education through free TED Talks, YouTube videos and online training programs. Knowledge is *almost never* the problem! However, our lack of knowledge is usually our excuse.

In my three years as a fitness manager, I found knowledge to be people's number one excuse. People would come in and make the case that they hadn't achieved their health and fitness goals because they didn't know where to start. Typically this isn't true. Pretty much everyone knows that if they eat more vegetables, drink more water, eat less junk food, and move more, they will lose weight. They usually (although not always) don't need a trainer to show them twenty-five complex exercises they have never seen and will never do again after their sessions are used up. What they really need is someone who can help them find a way to consistently take action on what they already know. Until we understand that a lack of knowledge is rarely the problem, we will use it as an excuse not to act.

This is where we separate those who are serious from those who are seeking success and accomplishment for the wrong reasons; those who are simply striving to get rich quick. The reason get-rich-quick plans don't typically work is that they

Until we understand that a lack of knowledge is rarely the problem, we will use it as an excuse not to act.

usually require much more sustained action than people are willing to invest. My desire for a nice car is not enough motivation for me to get up early and stay up late year after year. However, my passion to become a coach who can help people and organizations achieve their potential and maximize their impact in the world is. Belief is the fuel for action; therefore, you have to have a very deep belief in the importance of your vision in order to create enough leverage to act continuously.

In David Allen's book, *Getting Things Done*, he writes that we really only have two types of problems in life. Either we don't know where we are going, or we don't know how to get there. I would add one more critical problem, which is that we can't figure out how to make ourselves do what it takes to get there. This problem is typically overlooked and unaccounted for—which means people don't spend enough time trying to figure out solutions to this problem. This is where I spend a lot time with most of my coaching clients. When they figure this out, everything changes!

"Pray as though everything depended on God. Work as though everything depended on you."

—Saint Augustine

Key Chapter Takeaways:

1. Having a great vision and a well-thought-out plan doesn't mean you will be a guaranteed success. Every successful business leader knows that *execution is everything!*

2. Knowledge is *almost never* the problem, but our lack of knowledge is usually our excuse. Stop using that excuse today!

3. Action is the great differentiator! Action is what separates the people who make it to the top and the countless souls scattered along the path bloodied and beaten down by the challenges of life.

13

Mindset Matters

"A man's mind may be likened to a garden, which may be intelligently cultivated or allowed to run wild; but whether cultivated or neglected, it must, and will, bring forth."

—James Allen

IN THE YEARS I HAVE SPENT coaching and consulting others, I have found that systems and processes are essential to success, but they only work if there is a healthy mindset underneath them. It is our psychology—our beliefs, mindset, and attitudes—that drives our behaviors and whether we even decide to create systems in the first place. If we create them, our psychology influences whether we ever actually use them.

This chapter is focused on the areas you need to master first before the subsequent systems and strategies in the following chapter can truly add adequate value and actually move the needle in your life.

I am going to talk about three essential elements of an effective mindset that I believe will help shift your behavior toward action and success: desire, belief, and identity.

Desire

"When you want to succeed as bad as you want to breathe, then you'll be successful."

—Eric Thomas

Charles Wilson, former CEO of General Motors and former US secretary of defense, once said, "The thing that contributes to anyone's reaching the goal he wants is simply wanting that goal badly enough." If you really want to take your life to the next level, you have to find your *desire*! It can't be a surface-level desire—it must be the deepest that your soul can muster. The kind of passion you feel when you are in your peak state. The kind of excitement you feel when you watch your favorite emotion-stirring movie. Each of us has something that awakens our souls and speaks to our highest selves. Something that lights us up and transforms what we are willing to do and give.

I *know* you have felt this! I know if you slow down as you read this right now, you want a life fueled by desire. I'm also sure that, like me, you have a hard time tapping into that on a daily basis. As I am writing this, I am listening to motivational videos in the background, and I just heard speaker Eric Thomas say, "When you find your why, you don't hit snooze no more. When you find your why, you find a way to make it happen." It is so true! Let it sink in. You must understand the importance of your desire and how it motivates your actions. Desire is the gasoline of our lives! It fuels our actions to take us to the next level.

Zig Ziglar once said, "People often say that motivation doesn't last. Well, neither does bathing—that's why we recommend it daily." Some people think motivation isn't important because it doesn't carry you forever. While I do agree that motivation is often overrated, it still has its place.

If I watch the movie *Jobs*, about Steve Jobs, and it motivates me to stay up until 2:00 a.m. pursuing my goal, and the next day the motivation is gone, that's okay. It still got me to increase my effectiveness and play big that night. It still got me to make bold moves and drive hard for a short time. I have done that many times with that movie before its effect wore off on me. Before that, it was the movie *Steve Jobs* with Ashton Kutcher, and before that it was *The Social Network* about Mark Zuckerberg.

Every book, video, or tool that motivates me wears off eventually, so I am constantly searching for new content and stories that awaken me to bring my best self. I don't throw it all away saying that it didn't last so it wasn't worth it. When I watch the movie *Rocky*, my workout that night is killer. The next day it is back to normal. So what! Take the victory that night. Find ways to cultivate your desire and bring it to the surface consistently. Maybe it's a movie, maybe it's a song, maybe it's a cause. Whatever it is for you, find it, use it, and let it make you better. Remember my motto from chapter 4: "Intensity is great, but consistency is king." Even though I believe consistency is king, notice that intensity is still great. Even in short bursts, intensity can and will improve your life.

The bottom line is that your desire has to be incredibly strong to spur consistent and faithful action. No matter what your dream is, the journey ahead is filled with many challenges that will derail you if you aren't all in.

John Maxwell said, "Successful and unsuccessful people do not vary greatly in their abilities. They vary in their desires to reach their potential." Try to think of a handful of people in your life who, on a consistent basis, demonstrate a crazy desire to achieve their biggest dreams. You may find that not many people come to mind immediately. It is more rare than it is common. I love when something is rare, because it means if you embody it, you can differentiate yourself easier and separate yourself from the competition.

Desire spurs consistency, and consistency is king. Few things will help you in life like consistency, which is why I spent an entire chapter on it earlier in the book. Desire is the lifeblood of consistency. People who don't know how to tap into their passions deeply rarely maintain steady progress.

If, after reading this section, you realize you need a serious wake-up call, I have created a one-page worksheet for you in figure 4 that you can use to help identify your number one desire and then find ways to continually fuel yourself to reach it.

What are the three results you want most in life right now?

1. _____

2. _____

3. _____

Why do you want them? (What will they give you? How will they make you feel? What doors will they open for you?)

1. _____

_____

_____

2. _____

_____

_____

3. _____

_____

_____

Figure 4: *Desire Worksheet*

"There is one quality which one must possess to win, and that is definiteness of purpose—the knowledge of what one wants and a burning desire to possess it."

—Napoleon Hill

Belief

"I have always thought the actions of men the best interpreters of their thoughts."

—John Locke

Belief truly is the fuel for action. When our belief is weak, our action fades. I told you earlier that belief is at the very heart of the Peak Performance Cycle because it is so essential to the equation. If you don't think something is possible or worth it with every ounce of your heart and soul, you won't have the staying power to endure all the hardships and obstacles that will inevitably come your way. Belief is one of the most essential components of peak performance. There are three key elements:

1. Belief in what's possible
2. Belief in others
3. Belief in yourself

All three elements are crucial if you want to achieve success and impact at the highest levels in life. Look around and you will find these elements in people who have achieved great success and impact for the world. Think about Martin Luther King Jr. His belief in what's possible led him to declare a dream that seemed like an impossibility to most at the time. His belief in himself led him to consistently speak powerfully in front of thousands of people and lead through immense challenges and turmoil, and his belief in others ignited a movement that changed the world forever.

Belief is the fuel for action.

We all carry both empowering beliefs and limiting beliefs. The key is to identify your beliefs in both categories and find ways to eliminate the limiting ones and maximize the empowering ones. To help you progress in this area, I have created a one-page worksheet for you to start the process of creating and fueling the beliefs you need to achieve your dreams. See figure 5.

"Beliefs have the power to create and the power to destroy. Human beings have the awesome ability to take any experience of their lives and create a meaning that disempowers them or one that can literally save their lives."

—Tony Robbins

Identity

Our identities are one of the most powerful molders of our actions and behaviors on a daily basis. The way we view ourselves shapes who we become and how we live our lives. Unfortunately, our subconscious thoughts and unconscious habits are playing a huge role in the formation of those identities. In his book, *The Way We're Working Isn't Working*, author Tony Schwartz says, "For better and for worse, we are deeply creatures of habit. Fully ninety-five percent of our behavior occurs out of habit. Either unconsciously, or in reaction to external demands. We are run by the automatic processes of the primitive parts of our brain far more than we rely on the complex conscious capacities of our prefrontal cortex. In short, we think we are in charge of our lives but often we're not." These daily subconscious thoughts and behaviors play a significant role in the development of our identities, and therefore continue to shape our actions. We have a startling number of thoughts we don't even realize we are

What are your top three empowering beliefs? (Example: "I'm a lion—always willing to do whatever it takes to achieve my dreams.")

1. _____

2. _____

3. _____

What are your top three limiting beliefs? (Example: "I'm too old to achieve my dreams and become the person I hoped I would be.")

1. _____

2. _____

3. _____

Why are your limiting beliefs untrue? (Example: "I'm too old to achieve my dreams and become the person I hoped I would be." I have plenty of gas left in the tank! Harland "Colonel" Sanders was sixty-two when he franchised Kentucky Fried Chicken.)

1. _____

   _____

2. _____

   _____

3. _____

   _____

Figure 5: *Beliefs Worksheet*

having. These thoughts shape how we operate in our relationships, jobs, and daily life. The beauty of this, though, is that it means we also have the power to shape these subconscious thoughts. I believe molding our identities is one of the most powerful ways to change our ongoing behavior.

We hear parents and teachers talk about this often. If we tell a kid they are a troublemaker or a bad kid, often they will live into that identity. One of the strongest pulls we have as humans is to live consistently with our identities, and we will do that whether those identities are healthy or unhealthy. If you regularly call a child a liar, they will likely become more dishonest than they already were. Former Super Bowl champion NFL coach Jimmy Johnson said, "Treat a person as he is, and he will remain as he is. Treat him as he could be, and he will become what he should be." We should think about this in how we interact with others, but also in how we interact with ourselves.

Think of someone you know who has tried fad diet after fad diet for over a decade. Each time they start a new one, I would argue that even though outwardly they may be excited and think, *This is the one!*, inwardly and subconsciously, they are probably convinced that this time will be just like all the others. The serial dieter's identity is so deeply ingrained in their repeated failures that they really go in with the self-fulfilling prophecy that nothing will be different this time.

Once you understand this role of identity in your work as a coach, trainer, nutritionist, parent, or spouse, it gives you the ability to eliminate that root belief and create a new, empowering belief in its place. You should do this with yourself frequently. Find root identities that you no longer want and get rid of them. Do you identify yourself as someone who is always late? If so, your subconscious will work against you and you will likely continue to find yourself arriving late. If it bothers you and you want to change it, you have the ability to consciously choose what new identity you want—and find ways to reinforce the new and tear down the old.

Here are three easy steps you can take to eliminate an old identity and replace it with a new one. This is not a comprehensive list, but just a good place to start:

1. Write down the old identity and every reason you no longer want this to be true for you, or why it never was true. (Some identities we hold aren't accurate and are simply placed on us through other people's judgments or our own insecurities.)
2. Write down the new identity you want to replace it with and all the reasons this is important to you.
3. Place healthy reminders of your new identity in key areas you will see often. These can be photos, quotes, scripture, or anything that helps reinforce the importance of your new identity.

I identify myself as a disciplined person. I believe discipline is a very important key to success, and I try to differentiate myself through it. Because I still struggle with discipline at times, though, I try different approaches to help reinforce that identity. In the mornings on weekdays I take military showers, meaning I turn the water on, get wet, turn it off, soap and shampoo up, and then rinse off. As much as I love the environment and saving water, I actually do this because it reinforces my identity that I live a life filled with disciplined practices. As silly as this is, I have multiple habits like this and am willing to use whatever drives results in my life. My phone also has an alert set three times a day that says, "Fierce discipline, intense passion, relentless belief," to drive home three core identities I want to strengthen within me.

"If you're not willing to starve for your dreams, you're not worthy to eat from them."

—Noah Schultz

Key Chapter Takeaways:

1. If you really want to take your life to the next level, you have to find your desire! It can't be a surface-level desire—it must be the deepest that your soul can muster.

2. Belief is the fuel for action. When our belief is strong, our action is consistent. When our belief is weak, our action fades. There are three key elements: belief in what's possible, belief in others, belief in yourself.

3. One of the strongest pulls we have as humans is to live consistently with our identities, and we will do that whether those identities are healthy or unhealthy. Make sure you are constantly crafting healthy identities for yourself.

Tools and Tactics

"Systems always beat intentions."

—Lou Radja

FINALLY, IT'S TIME to get to work and implement systems and practices that will concretely change your behavior and help you get closer to the life you desire. If you have taken the time to work through the mindset worksheets from the last chapter, you will have a huge advantage and will be much more likely to utilize the tools presented in this chapter.

I have seen systems and processes drive incredible results in countless people and organizations. Almost everyone has great intentions. On their wedding day, everyone intends to stay married for the rest of their lives. Everyone intends to be a good parent. Most people intend on reaching their full potential and becoming all they are capable of becoming, but few even come close to living up to their intentions. Almost none. When you see a gap between someone's intentions and their actions, you can usually find a gap in their systems and processes. If you're one of these people, there is likely a system

When you see a gap between someone's intentions and their actions, you can usually find a gap in their systems and processes.

that, if implemented effectively, can change the behavior you so desperately want to change.

In this chapter, I talk about a few key tools and systems that will help you minimize the gaps between where you are and where you want to be, and between who you are and who you want to be.

Leverage

"You have heard that necessity is the mother of invention. Well, necessity is also the mother of accomplishment."

—Joey Jenkins

Yes, I just quoted myself. I don't like to do that, even though I love to create quotes! But in this case, I think this quote is important since the example I am going to give is personal. Let me tell you a quick story that is at the heart of this book: how I overcame my snooze-button addiction.

After nine years of having a strong desire to stop hitting the snooze button, I finally realized I was missing a crucial strategy that could help me win in this area. As we know by now, desire by itself isn't enough. So I came up with an approach, which ended up being a lot simpler than I thought it would be (it almost always is when it comes to changing a habit).

Before I landed on that winning strategy, I tried everything to kick the habit! (Not really. People often think they have tried everything when usually we have only tried a couple of things.) I tried:

- Accountability check-ins from friends: These helped sometimes for a few months, but ultimately the person forgot, I forgot, and I fell back into the same old habits.

- Tapping into my drive and motivation, my *why*: This rarely worked, as my motivation was much lower at 5:00 a.m.

Finally, I implemented a tool called leverage, which I have used many times since and it still helps me regularly accomplish my goals.

Often if we don't have what we want in life, it is simply because there is not enough leverage to give us the discipline and focus we need to achieve it.

Imagine you were told the terrible news that if you couldn't make an additional $100,000 each year, you would not be able to afford a critical life-saving drug for one of your children who is sick. Pretty much every parent out there could find a way to do this instantly. They would beg, borrow, or steal their way to success! Even if they have "wanted" to achieve that goal prior to the child's diagnosis but have been unsuccessful in accomplishing it, they would suddenly become more disciplined, creative, and resourceful to find a way.

Now, don't get me wrong, this doesn't mean everyone should think like that all the time, because creating false leverage where it truly doesn't exist can cause people to violate their morals and values. Look at the scandals related to Enron in 2001, Lehman Brothers in 2008, and Wells Fargo in 2017, just to name a few. Be careful when and where you use this tool, but use it occasionally to leverage the results and success you want in all areas of your life.

Let me give two examples of how I used this powerful tool to achieve my desired result. One example was used for project-based results, and the other was used for habit-based results.

Project-Based Leverage
About a year into my business, I still didn't have a website and I desperately wanted one. I knew it would make me feel more competent and credible, and would also give me a place to market my services.

However, I also didn't have many financial resources to hire this out and am not tech savvy at all. It was a really overwhelming project for me.

On one of my coaching calls with esteemed business coach David Brownlee, he questioned how high of a priority it was for me to get my website up in comparison to everything else in my business. I told him it was my number one priority. He then asked me if it was *possible* in the next two weeks to do the research, put in the time, and use the finances I needed to have my website up if I *really committed* to it. Knowing where we were going, I reluctantly said yes, because although it hadn't felt possible for me yet, I knew it was.

Then Brownlee did something crazy and unheard of to me at the time. He asked me who was my least favorite person I could think of. Someone who really rubbed me wrong. I generally like most people, so it took a minute to think of someone, but then that one challenging person popped into my mind. He then responded by suggesting that I commit to writing that person a check for $500 with no explanation but a simple note in the memo line that said, *For being such a great guy*, if my website wasn't launched by our next call two weeks later.

My first reaction was to tell him he was crazy, that my wife would kill me, and that it would be too embarrassing to write that person a check for that much money. You know what he told me? "Then simply don't let it happen."

Long story short, he got me to make the commitment, and two weeks later my website was up! Just like that. When the stakes were high enough, I figured out a way to make it happen! As soon as I hung up the phone with him, I locked in ten time blocks in my schedule to work on it, set multiple reminders, and made a few phone calls to figure out the easiest path to achieve my goal.

If you have a project on your backlog that you've been longing to complete, I challenge you to take a minute right now and create some form of leverage for yourself. Test this principle, and I am confident you will be pleasantly surprised with the result. But in order for it

Business coach David Brownlee and me at
Brendon Burchard's Experts Academy.

to work, you have to commit to sticking with the result, no matter what! If I had failed, I would have written that check, no matter how painful and embarrassing it would have been.

Habit-Based Leverage

Example number two is how I finally conquered (let's say *managed*, to not jinx it) my snooze- button problem.

I finally hit my wall—I was fed up with not being the most disciplined, focused, and committed person I could be. I picked up the phone and made a call to my older and wiser brother, Chris. That is when I made a simple commitment to him, which I then outlined in a one-page lifelong contract:

Snooze Button Contract

This contract was created to ensure Joey Jenkins achieves a life worthy of the call he has received. It is his commitment to never forget the power and importance of the "little things" in life. To always remember the law of compounding interest and how it applies to all areas of life. Discipline and consistency are the keys to achieving success in all areas. How you do one thing is how you do everything!

The Rule:
1. Joey will not hit the snooze button and must wake up and not go back to bed at the sound of his first alarm.
   a. Exceptions
      i. If Joey wakes up sick and can tell that more sleep might prevent or expedite his recovery, he may hit the snooze button in **extreme circumstances only**.
      ii. If Joey accidentally had his alarm set, but had no intention of waking up at that time the night before. This should be **extremely** rare.

Punishment
1. If Joey violates this contract he will be required under law to donate $10 to the charity of Chris Jenkins' choosing. The donation must be made within 72 hours of the violation with no exceptions regardless of financial circumstance.
   a. The charity cannot be Ncompass or any other charity Joey works for or heavily volunteers for.

Length of Contract
1. This contract will expire the day that Joey dies.
   a. The only other way for this contract to end is by mutual agreement by both Chris and Joey.

Joey Jenkins (signature): _____ Date: 6-10-14

Chris Jenkins (signature): _____ Date: 6.10.14

*Me with my older brother, Chris—one of my
greatest role models, mentors, and my best
friend.*

The contract didn't work immediately. In the first two months, I hit the snooze button three times (still way better than my habit previously). I donated $10 each time to the Boys & Girls Club at his request. After the third time, I realized my wife probably wouldn't be happy with me bleeding us dry through micro donations for a few extra minutes of sleep. My wife and I are huge believers in giving to charities, especially ones empowering youth like the Boys & Girls Club. We believe you can't out-give God and that you will always receive exponentially more than you actually give, though not always in monetary currency. It was the principle that this was money we weren't choosing to give. The only reason I specified the funds to go to charity in the first place was because I was afraid I wouldn't break my habit and I would be giving a lot of money over the years, so I thought I should at least make it go to a good cause.

It doesn't have to be a charitable donation though. I have coached people to financially support a sports team they hate when they fail to meet a commitment. I had a friend and former Oregon State graduate writing many $50 checks to the University of Oregon Athletic Department every time they failed to live up to their own contractual commitment. Leverage can be tweaked to whatever will work best for you.

To finish the story and show you where I landed in this journey, the last time I hit the snooze button was in August of 2014, and today is April 27th, 2018.

So there's my snooze-button success story and how you can use leverage to help you achieve success in specific habits or projects you haven't been able to master yet.

Now you may be wondering, *But, Joey, has it changed your life drastically?* No, unfortunately not. That is the beautiful and unfortunate part of this all. Usually the small changes we make in life don't produce instant results. The day I stopped hitting the snooze button, I didn't get a call from an investor saying, "Hey, I heard about you and your relentless drive and focus to get better. I would like to invest $1 million in your business and give another million to your nonprofit organization." I think this is what we all secretly hope will happen to us, even though when we read it, it sounds ridiculous.

Deep down, I think this is why most people fail to do the little things on a consistent basis. The reward or punishment doesn't come instantly. If it did, everyone would do the little things. It's not like touching a stove when you are a little kid (which I still vividly remember doing). Typically, you touch that stove once, and it is burned (literally) in your memory that it was a poor choice! You don't make the same mistake again.

Unfortunately, in life the punishment for not doing the little things doesn't usually come for years. When you don't save money every month, you don't instantly become homeless and destitute. You don't notice any negative side effects for decades sometimes. Then suddenly when you are sixty years old, you realize you will have to work until you are eighty, and that thought can be extremely overwhelming.

When you don't exercise multiple times a week, you don't die of a heart attack after the first week of failing to show up to the gym, but after some time, maybe twenty years, you have a fatal heart attack that leaves your wife and three children alone. If you had been exercising or eating better, you might have lived another thirty years and been there to walk your daughter down the aisle or hold your grandson for the first time. The artery doesn't harden overnight. It's the slow buildup of plaque over decades that leads to that one fatal moment we all dread. One cheeseburger doesn't make the difference, but decades of poor choices compounded over time do.

On the flip side, when you do those little things well, you don't see instant results. The day you decide to sponsor a child's education in Haiti, you don't see right away who that child becomes as a result of your educational support. You don't get to see her work her way through school, become a wife, mother, teacher, and eventually the principal of a school. You don't get to see her train and develop amazing teachers who love kids and have incredible character and integrity. You don't get to see all the kids she educates in the future become productive members of society contributing in powerful and beautiful ways. These events don't unfold overnight. It usually takes time and patience to see the fruit of our labor. There is power and magic in the little things! Never underestimate them.

Become a man or woman of great patience and willingness to plant seeds, water them for years, and wait for them to bear fruit. I promise no overnight results, but I guarantee you will never regret doing the little things over decades if you can wait and stay persistent.

Positive and Negative Reinforcement

Positive and negative reinforcement can be very powerful ways to drive behavior. They were discussed briefly in the snooze-button example of leverage, but I believe they need a little more depth here.

Economics 101 says people respond to incentives. Whether an incentive should be a carrot or a stick is typically situational. The carrot usually drives better, longer-lasting results when used effectively, but there are also plenty of situations when the stick works as well (as demonstrated by my snooze button contract).

Positive Reinforcement

Modern research encourages positive reinforcement as the more effective and beneficial incentive of the two. However, this method is difficult to implement well, especially when our society regularly pushes us on to the next task immediately. From my experience in the corporate world as well as years of consulting, the most common complaint I hear from employees is that their bosses don't celebrate them enough. We complain about this regarding our bosses, but then we do the exact same thing to ourselves. We live in a "What's next?" society. Once we accomplish our goal, we pause for about two seconds and then jump right into the next task. There are benefits to this, but there is also a dark side to it. We rarely let the accomplishments sink in. We don't pause for long enough to celebrate, release the endorphins, let the accomplishment build our identity, and harness the motivation to effectively launch that next big project.

Brendon Burchard covered this topic extensively during a 2016 conference I attended. He recommended we take every critical project of ours and create five key milestones for it, then attach some sort of reward or celebration to each milestone.

Let's say John wants to write his first book but has been putting it off for the past five years. It isn't urgent, and he just never makes the time (notice I said *makes* vs. *finds*). Figure 6 is an example of what he can do to change course, take action, and finally get that book done and published.

The positive reinforcement helps John have both intrinsic and extrinsic motivation to get his book done. Now he is not only motivated by his desire to get his content into thousands of people's hands to drive deep impact in society (intrinsic motivation), but he

Overall Goal: Complete First Book

Milestone	Deadline	Reward (If Successful)
Create outline	January 15th	Smoothie date with wife
Complete sloppy draft one	March 31st	Guys' night out
Complete refined draft two	June 30th	Dinner with wife at nicest restaurant in the city
Thorough edit and refinement	September 30th	New set of golf clubs
Publish final draft	December 31st	Trip to Europe to celebrate

Figure 6: *An example of five key milestones and rewards.*

is also motivated by that exciting dinner date with his wife, a new set of clubs, and an incredible trip to Europe (extrinsic motivation). Some days the intrinsic motivation is enough, but some days it is that set of golf clubs that just might get John to crank out a few chapters.

Negative Reinforcement

While I agree with most researchers that negative reinforcement is not as effective as positive reinforcement, it can still have a place as a very effective tool to drive results in our lives. Negative reinforcement is essentially a punishment for not meeting your desired goal or behavior, just as I had in my snooze button contract. Let's use the same example above with John and just replace his rewards with punishments instead. See figure 7.

This is obviously just a generic list to give you some potential ideas. Different rewards and punishments will be more effective for specific types of people. You really need to know yourself well and think through these incentives thoroughly to ensure they are healthy, drive the result you want, and help you achieve your end outcome without destructive negative side effects.

Overall Goal: Complete First Book

Milestone	Deadline	Punishment (If Failed)
Create outline	January 15th	Watch *The Sound of Music* with your wife
Complete sloppy draft one	March 31st	Write $100 check to rival sports team's athletic department
Complete refined draft two	June 30th	Cancel guys' night out next month
Thorough edit and refinement	September 30th	Sell golf clubs
Publish final draft	December 31st	Buy tickets to Europe for your friend instead of yourself

Figure 7: *An example of five key milestones and punishments.*

My challenge to you is to give this process a shot and see if it can help you achieve a goal or finish a project that has been on your list for quite some time. In the space below, choose a project or goal you want to test this with, and fill in the information.

Goal or Project: _____

Milestone	Deadline	Reward/Punishment

Figure 8: *Key milestones worksheet.*

Scorecard

"What gets measured gets managed."

—Peter Drucker

When you study the most successful people in the world, you will probably find that they track most of their critical actions. CEOs have multiple KPIs (key performance indicators) they measure to drive success in what matters most in their business. Olympic athletes record how many calories they eat, how many they burn, and the intensity and duration of every workout. This is what it takes to become a peak performer. This is why I use scorecards to help me both in my business and my personal life. I also teach the clients I coach to use scorecards as well.

Every Monday morning, I send my personal scorecard to my old mentor, Troy Snow. During different seasons I have sent a business/marketing scorecard to my good friend Jonathan Reed for strategy and accountability support in my business. Our nonprofit Ncompass also has a one-page scorecard the Executive Director sends our board monthly to ensure we drive key behaviors.

I have attached two examples to give you an idea of what this can look like. You should occasionally modify these documents depending on the season and stage of life you are in and what needs tracking the most.

You can use this tool however serves you best if it makes sense in your line of work.

Scorecards can help you in a variety of ways:

1. They drive focus in the areas that matter most.
2. They help you build momentum on new habits you wish to install. Then you can slowly phase them out of the scorecard once they become consistent and as easy as brushing your teeth.

3. They enable you be intentional about your upcoming week and live in line with your core values and key priorities.

Author and financial educator, Dave Ramsey, often says, "If you will live like no one else, later you can live like no one else." Think about that for a minute. How badly do you want to win? How much do you want to live the life you have dreamed of and feel called to? What are you willing to sacrifice to create the impact you are capable of? To most people, this may seem like way too much effort to put in the time and focus. But most people never achieve peak performance either.

I have found that without proper support and training, most people will quit using the scorecard within a month. The most common reason for this is that it can be a very discouraging practice if you don't go into it with the right mindset. It is hard to see a scorecard with a score of 47/100. It is fairly common to have low scores because we are overly ambitious as well as the fact that it simply takes time to instill new habits and practices. I believe that in order for a scorecard to be truly effective, you have to continually ask yourself one simple question: "Am I doing more of what matters to me because of the scorecard than I would be doing without it?" Usually the answer is yes. Even if you get a 47/100 on your personal scorecard, typically it will have gotten you to improve in at least one key area or behavior. As long as you can focus on the improvement and not let the gap overwhelm you, this can be a life-changing practice.

Goal Setting

One of my favorite tools for getting you from where you are to where you want to be—and from who you are to who you want to be—faster, is goal setting. It's one of those tactics that almost everyone agrees is good to do, but almost no one does.

Many people reading this might think they are goal setters because they come up with one resolution each year in January. How-

Weekly Scorecard

Week	Scoring Key	May 7th	May 14th
Morning Routine (5x per week at 2 pts each)	10	8	6
Night Routine (5x per week at 2 pts each)	10	6	8
Green Drink (5x per week at 1 pt each)	5	4	3
Salad (3x per week at 1 pt each)	3	3	2
Lemon Water (1x per week at 2 pts)	2	2	2
Chia Seed Water (1x per wk at 2 pts)	2	2	0
One Set of Pushups (5x per week at 1 pt each)	5	4	5
One Set of Pullups (5x per week at 1 pt each)	5	4	5
One Minute Plank (5x per week at 1 pt each)	5	4	5
Serving of Olives (1x per wk at 2 pts)	2	2	0
Serving of Fish (1x per wk at 3 pts)	3	0	3
Exercise (6x per week at 6 pts each)	36	30	36
Walking 7,000 Steps Daily (6 days per week at 1 pt each)	6	4	5
7 Hours of Sleep Each Night (6 days per week at 1 pt each)	6	3	4
8 Hours of Sleep a Night = One Bonus Point	0	0	1
Total Score	**100**	**76**	**85**

Figure 9: *Example of a personal weekly scorecard.*

OPERATIONS	January	February	March	April	May	June	July	August	September	October	November	December
Goal % Completion	90%	85%	77%	76%	82%	88%	83%	77%	89%	95%	90%	80%
Meeting Attendance	9	11	8	10	8	10	8	10	7	6	6	5
Timeline Review	1/12/17	2/24/17	3/29/17	4/28/17	5/31/17	6/30/17	7/28/17	8/29/17	9/30/17	Missed	11/30/17	12/20/17
Financial Review	1/6/17	2/10/17	3/15/17	4/17/17	5/19/17	Missed	7/23/17	8/15/17	n/a	10/10/17	11/7/17	12/17/17
Facebook Likes	2,319	3,043	3,078	3,109	3,233	3,455	3,765	4,117	4,287	4,555	5,709	7,011
Instagram Followers	432	486	522	577	612	636	693	719	801	865	902	978
Twitter Followers	350	410	473	510	545	592	613	652	697	727	763	809
Blog Posts	2	3	4	3	4	4	4	3	4	4	2	4
Thank You's To Customers	24	11	32	15	79	6	27	65	11	14	170	86
Employee Gifts	2	3	2	1	4	2	7	1	2	3	2	17

Figure 10: *Example of a yearlong business scorecard.*

ever, that is not even close to the kind of goal setting I'm talking about—or the kind of goal setting that actually drives results in your life. Others may wander around with a few aspirations bouncing around in their heads from time to time, but that doesn't yield results for most people either. In his book *The Way We're Working Isn't Working*, author Tony Schwartz highlights how ineffective simple goal setting that stops at New Year's resolutions can be. He says, "Twenty-five percent of people abandon their New Year's resolutions after one week. Sixty percent do so within six months. The average person makes the same New Year's resolution ten separate times without success." Clearly another, more effective form of goal setting is worth trying.

For those few of you out there who don't believe in the power of goal setting, I'd like to feature a few people here to try to convince you to the contrary:

- "I'm a firm believer in goal setting. Step by step. I can't see any other way of accomplishing anything." Michael Jordan
- "You are never too old to set another goal or to dream a new dream." C. S. Lewis
- "If you're bored with life—you don't get up every morning with a burning desire to do things—you don't have enough goals." Lou Holtz

Once you believe in the power of goal setting, the next step is to learn how to do it most effectively. Goal setting is about creating measurable targets that will improve the most important areas of your life. It's about creating a system and process that you can stick to so you can accomplish those critical targets. There are dangerous and ineffective ways to do this, as well as powerful and productive ways.

I wasn't much of a goal setter until I was nineteen years old. It was the book I mentioned earlier, *Slaying the Dragon* by Michael

Johnson, that awakened my desire to not simply be a dreamer but to also be a doer. For the last fourteen years, I have been a diligent goal setter and have seen and felt the impact in my life in many key areas.

Let me first talk about some of the mistakes I have made in my goal-setting process over the years and give you some key actions *not* to do:

1. Don't set too many goals.
2. Don't write your goals down but not look at them again until their deadline.
3. Don't set too lofty of goals that leave you consistently feeling disappointed.
4. Don't forget to have consistent outside accountability.

For those of you who want to ensure this year is your best year yet, here are my four tips for successful goal setting:

1. **Create SMARTER goals:** The acronym, which lays the foundation for goal setting 101, stands for: Specific, Measurable, Attainable, Realistic, Time bound, Evaluate, and Revise. This is a great formula for setting goals that are likely to actually move the needle in your life. Not all goals have to follow the SMARTER system, but most should.
2. **Make them exciting:** This is one important aspect the SMARTER acronym leaves out. When you envision accomplishing your goals at the end of the year, what you see should really energize you, and provide enough motivation to get up early and stay up late when necessary. Remember Simon Sinek's message: Your goals need to have a strong *why* and a real purpose behind them if you are going to have enough grit and resilience to make them happen.

Exhilarating goals tap into that *why*, which gives them more meaning and purpose.

3. **Share them with others:** I have multiple people I share my goals with every week and month. There are two great benefits in doing this. First, we all need accountability. Sharing your goals with others gives you more leverage to make them happen. I have found that I accomplish the goals I share with others at a much higher percentage than I do the goals I keep to myself. The second benefit to sharing with others is it gives us other people to celebrate with when we win. As human beings, we thrive off shared experiences. It is why we usually watch sporting events together instead of alone. Having someone else to celebrate with makes accomplishing a goal much more exhilarating!

4. **Celebrate early and often:** As I mentioned before, we live in a "What's next?" society. We hit one goal and just move right on to the next. We're always looking at the next mountain to climb and obstacle to overcome. There is some good in this, but we also need to pause and celebrate the wins every once in a while. For this reason, I often create rewards attached to hitting specific goals as demonstrated earlier in this chapter. For larger projects, I create rewards at multiple milestones.

Hopefully some of these tips help you avoid the goal-setting blunders I used to experience. I will leave you with another quote by Denzel Washington: "Dreams without goals remain dreams, just dreams, and ultimately fuel disappointment." Go out and make some magic happen this year!

"Watch the little things; a small leak will sink a great ship."

—Benjamin Franklin

Key Chapter Takeaways:

1. Leverage is one of the most powerful tools to drive behavior. If you have a project on your backlog that you've been longing to complete, I challenge you to take a minute right now and create some form of leverage for yourself.
2. When you study the most successful people in the world, you will find that they track most of their critical actions. As Peter Drucker says, "What gets measured gets managed."
3. Goal setting is one of the most powerful tools to improve all areas of your life. Write them down and share them with a friend to drastically increase your likelihood of success.

CONCLUSION

"You cannot change your destination overnight, but you can change your direction overnight."

—Jim Rohn

MY HOPE FOR YOU as you finish this book is that you have gained some inspiration, encouragement, and tools that will help you break through in critical areas in your life. Don't expect overnight results. Make the commitment today to start taking advantage of the small habits and behaviors that can and will change your life. Once that commitment has been made and you start taking action, wait patiently for the results to come. All great things in life take time.

I know the tools, strategies, and systems I have outlined in this book may not be for everyone. That's okay. Take what works for you and discard the rest. I only care that you take action in the areas that are truly going to make a real difference for you and the areas that matter most to you. If an idea, system, or habit I recommended isn't for you, just make sure you have that area dialed or you find another tool that will yield the outcome it was supposed to achieve.

One small habit I find useful when I'm reading books is to summarize the key takeaways as I read. This helps me to easily refer back to what resonated most with me and then take action in important areas. Here is a place you can make notes on the top ideas you want to remember and the core actions you want to implement:

Three key philosophies or mindsets I will remember from this book:

1. _____

2. _____

3. _____

Three key actions I will start doing as a result of this book:

1. _____

2. _____

3. _____

If this book hasn't delivered for you, and did not achieve the goals I laid out in the beginning, then here are my email and phone number: joey@optimalimpactgroup.com, 503-680-0790. Contact me, and I will personally apologize to you, because I know time is our most precious asset. If the book did positively impact you, then go out and do something with it! Don't sit back, and don't waste what you learned. Apply it and use it, and then go model and teach it to others so we can all lift each other up and raise the standards around us.

The magic is in the little things! It is the little things that will either give you that breakthrough or prohibit it. Breakthrough is what we all desperately want and need. We need a mental breakthrough to make the radical leap and start that business. We need a physical breakthrough to hit our 5K running personal record. We need an emotional breakthrough to fall back in love with our spouse who we

Conclusion

committed to spending the rest of our lives with. The list goes on and on. I am here to tell you that with consistent, focused action, breakthrough is coming. With consistent, focused action, breakthrough is inevitable. Please don't ever give up and don't ever give in. And please, please, please...

Never hit the snooze button again!

All my best!
—Joey

BIBLIOGRAPHY

Adevey, Alesike Gladys. *The Best of You: Nurtured Hand is a Fulfilled Life*. Bloomington: Authorhouse, 2012.

Allen, David. *Getting Things Done: The Art of Stress-Free Productivity*. Read by the author. New York: Simon and Schuster Audio, 2016. Audible audio ed., 10 hr., 29 min.

Berardino, Mike. "Mike Tyson Explains One of His Most Famous Quotes." *The Sun Sentinel*, November 9, 2012. http://articles.sun-sentinel.com/2012-11-09/sports/sfl-mike-tyson-explains-one-of-his-most-famous-quotes-20121109_1_mike-tyson-undisputed-truth-famous-quotes

Brown, Brené. *Rising Strong: How the Ability to Reset Transforms the Way We Live, Love, Parent, and Lead*. Read by the author. New York: Random House Audio, 2015. Audible audio ed., 8 hr., 50 min.

Carter, Ben. "Can 10,000 Hours of Practice Make You an Expert?" *BBC News*, March 1, 2014. http://www.bbc.com/news/magazine-26384712.

Coelho, Paulo. *The Alchemist*. New York: HarperCollins Publishers, 2005.

Covey, Sean, Chris McChesney, and Jim Huling. *The Four Disciplines of Execution: Achieving Your Wildly Important Goals*. New York: Free Press, 2012.

Drucker, Peter. *The Effective Executive: The Definitive Guide to Getting the Right Things Done*. Read by Jim Collins and Tim Andres Pabon. New York: HarperAudio, 2017. Audible audio ed., 6 hr., 15 min.

Drucker, Peter. *The Practice of Management*. New York: Harper & Row, 1954.

Ducey, Jake. *The Purpose Principles: How to Draw More Meaning into Your Life*. New York: The Penguin Group, 2015.

Dudley, Drew. "Everyday Leadership." Filmed 2010 in Toronto, ON. TEDx video, 6:11. https://www.ted.com/talks/drew_dudley_everyday_leadership

Durant, Will. *The Story of Philosophy*. New York: Simon and Schuster, 2012.

Dweck, Carol. *Mindset: The New Psychology of Success. How We Can Learn to Fulfill Our Potential*. Read by Marguerite Gavin., Gildan Media, 2009. Audible audio ed., 8 hr., 34 min.

Ferriss, Tim. *The 4-Hour Workweek: Escape 9-5, Live Anywhere, and Join the New Rich*. Crown Publishing Group, 2007.

FriendsofJeff.com. "About Jeff." Accessed May 11, 2018. http://www.friendsofjeff.com/Jeff.htm

Han, Anh. *Intention Recognition, Commitment and Their Roles in the Evolution of Cooperation: From Artificial Intelligence Techniques to Evolutionary Game Theory Models*. New York: Springer-Verlag Berlin Heidelberg, 2013.

Hardy, Darren. *The Compound Effect*. New York: Vanguard Press, 2011.

Bibliography

Harris, Alex, and Brett Harris. *Do Hard Things: A Teenage Rebellion against Low Expectations*. Sisters, OR: Multnomah, 2008.

History.com. "Notre Dame Beats UCLA to End 88-Game Winning Streak." This Day in History, January 19. Accessed May 10, 2018. https://www.history.com/this-day-in-history/notre-dame-beats-ucla-to-end-88-game-winning-streak

InsideOut Development. Alan Fine profile page. Accessed May 11, 2018. https://www.insideoutdev.com/about-us/alan-fine-keynote/

Johnson, Michael. *Slaying the Dragon: How to Turn Your Small Steps to Great Feats*. New York: HarperCollins Publishers, 1996.

Jordan, Michael. *I Can't Accept Not Trying: Michael Jordan on the Pursuit of Excellence*. San Francisco, CA: Harper San Francisco, 1994.

Keller, Gary, and Jay Papasan. *The One Thing: The Surprisingly Simple Truth behind Extraordinary Results*. Read by Timothy Miller and Claire Hamilton. Austin, TX: Bard Press, 2013. Audible audio ed., 5 hr., 28 min.

La Monica, Paul R. "Apple Inches Closer to $1 Trillion Market Value." *CNN Money*, May 7, 2018. http://money.cnn.com/2018/05/07/investing/apple-trillion-dollar-market-value/index.html

McKeown, Greg. *Essentialism: The Disciplined Pursuit of Less*. Read by the author., Random House Audio, 2014. Audible audio ed., 6 hr., 14 min.

McRaven, William. *Make Your Bed: Little Things That Can Change Your Life... And Maybe the World*. Read by the author., Grand Central Publishing, 2017. Audible audio ed., 1 hr., 44 min.

Morning-routine.com. "Famous and Successful People with Morning Routines." Accessed May 5, 2018. http://morning-routine.com/famous-and-successful-people-with-morning-routines/.

Navyseals.com. "SEAL Ethos." Accessed May 10, 2018. https://navyseals. com/ns-overview/seal-ethos/.

Networthleaks.com. "Gary Vaynerchuk's Net Worth (2018)." Accessed May 10, 2018. https://www.networthleaks.com/gary-vaynerchuk/

Olin, Ken, dir. *This Is Us.* Season 1, episode 18, "Moonshadow." Aired March 14, 2017, on NBC.

Olsen, Jeff. *The Slight Edge: Turning Simple Disciplines into Massive Success and Happiness.* Austin, TX: Greenleaf Book Group, 2013.

Page, Rick. *Hope Is Not a Strategy: The 6 Keys to Winning the Complex Sale.* New York: McGraw-Hill, 2002.

Pathak, Shareen. "#TheHustler: How Gary Vee Became the Ad Industry's Lightning Rod." *Digiday*, April 25, 2017. https://digiday.com/ marketing/thehustler-gary-vee-became-ad-industrys-lightning- rod/.

Rauf, Brian. "Who Has Won the Most NCAA Basketball Championships?" Chatsports.com, April 2, 2018. Accessed May 10, 2018. https:// www.chatsports.com/ncaa/a/who-has-won-most-ncaa-basketball- championships-32767

Reed, Jonathan, dir. *Perception: From Prison to Purpose.* Dream Big Act Small Media, 2017.

Robbins, Anthony. "Are Your Beliefs Holding You Back?" *Robbins Research International.*   https://www.tonyrobbins.com/stories/are-your- beliefs-holding-you-back/

Robbins, Anthony. *Giant Steps: Small Changes to Make a Big Difference. 365 Daily Lessons in Self-Mastery.* New York: Simon & Schuster, 1994.

Robbins, Anthony. "It's in your moments of decision that your destiny is shaped." Filmed July 2010. YouTube video, 4:19. https://www. youtube.com/watch?v=lFSxHyI7eOM

Bibliography

Robbins, Anthony. *Power Talk!: Raising Your Standards*. Read by the author. Rochester, NY: Audio Renaissance, n.d. Audiocassette.

Robbins, Mel. *The 5 Second Rule: Transform Your Life, Work, and Confidence with Everyday Courage*. Read by the author., Savio Republic, 2017. Audible audio ed., 7 hr., 36 min.

Schwartz, Tony, Jean Gomez and Catherine McCarthy, PH.D. *The Way We're Working Isn't Working: The Power of Full Engagement*. Read by the author., Simon &Schuster, 2010. Audible audio ed., 6 hr., 16 min.

Sinek, Simon. "How Great Leaders Inspire Action." Filmed September 2009 in Puget Sound, WA. TED video, 17:58. https://www.ted.com/talks/simon_sinek_how_great_leaders_inspire_action.

Snell, Jason. "Steve Jobs: Making a Dent in the Universe." *MacWorld*, October 6, 2011. https://www.macworld.com/article/1162827/macs/steve-jobs-making-a-dent-in-the-universe.html

"Sporting News Honors Wooden." ESPN.com, Associated Press, July 29, 2009. http://www.espn.com/mens-college-basketball/news/story?id=4365068

Stone, Oliver, dir. *Any Given Sunday*. Burbank, CA: Warner Bros., 1999.

"Think Different." Apple advertising campaign. Original air date September 1997. YouTube video, 1:09. https://www.youtube.com/watch?v=cFEarBzelBs

Thomas, Eric. "One of the Best Motivation Ever." Filmed January 2018. YouTube video, 36:33. https://www.youtube.com/watch?v=TuKlCOn8uFY&t=10s.

———. "Take Me to Your Bedroom..." Filmed March 2017. YouTube video, 5:19. https://www.youtube.com/watch?v=hY2jMNZz6N8.

Thompson, Mary. "It's 'a Disgrace': This Is How Much More CEOs Make Than Workers." CNBC, May 17, 2016. https://www.cnbc.com/2016/05/17/its-a-disgrace-this-is-how-much-more-ceos-make-than-workers.html

UCLA Newsroom. "Coach John Wooden Quotes." UCLA Anderson | John Wooden Global Leadership Award ceremony (May 21, 2009). http://newsroom.ucla.edu/releases/wooden-quotes-84178.

Vaynerchuk, Gary. "Overnight Success." Filmed October 2015. YouTube video, 7:59. https://www.youtube.com/watch?v=OTHbFb1fNy4

———. "The Ambition of a Human-Based Company." garyvaynerchuk.com, 2016. https://www.garyvaynerchuk.com/the-ambition-of-a-human-based-company/

Wealthygorilla.com. "Gary Vaynerchuk Net Worth." Accessed May 10, 2018. https://wealthygorilla.com/gary-vaynerchuk-net-worth/

Winley, Rich. "Business Plans: The Roadmap to Procrastination." *Forbes*, September 22, 2015. https://www.forbes.com/sites/richwinley/2015/09/22/business-plans-the-roadmap-to-procrastination/#7b7100df6e65.

Wooden, John, and Steve Jamison. *Wooden: A Lifetime Of Observations And Reflections On And Off The Court*. New York: McGraw-Hill, 1997.

Wooden, John, and Steve Jamison. *Wooden on Leadership*. New York: McGraw-Hill, 2005.

Ziglar, Zig. *Born to Win*. Seminar on CD and DVD. Nightingale Conant, 2010. https://www.ziglar.com/product/born-to-win/

———. *Raising Positive Kids in a Negative World*. New York: HarperCollins, 2002.